FEATURE ENGINEERING FOR THE WIN: BUILDING POWERFUL MODELS WITH THE RIGHT DATA

DR.N.KRISHNARAJ

Made with ♥ on the Notion Press Platform
www.notionpress.com

Contents

## CHAPTER ONE

INTRODUCTION

In the world of machine learning, where algorithms churn through massive datasets, the quality of the data fed to the model is paramount. While powerful algorithms can be impressive, even the most sophisticated model is only as good as the features it is trained on. This book, *Feature Engineering for the Win: Building Powerful Models with the Right Data,* introduces you to the art and science of feature engineering, the process of transforming raw data into meaningful attributes that a machine learning model can understand and leverage. We'll delve into the why and how of feature engineering, exploring how it can elevate your models from mediocre to masterful. By understanding your data, creating informative features, and selecting the most impactful ones, you'll unlock the true potential of your machine learning projects. This book equips you with a comprehensive toolbox of feature engineering techniques, from feature scaling and encoding categorical data to crafting powerful interaction features and reducing dimensionality for complex datasets. Whether you're tackling classification problems, building image recognition systems, or forecasting future trends, feature engineering will become your secret weapon for building robust and accurate models. So, if you're ready to transform your data from good to great and empower your machine learning models to achieve peak performance, dive into the pages of *Feature Engineering for the Win* and unleash the power of the right data. Data is the fuel that powers machine learning models, but just like a car won't run on raw gasoline, machine learning models can't function effectively on unprocessed information. This is where feature engineering comes in – the essential process of transforming raw data into meaningful features, the building blocks that models can understand and leverage for making predictions. This book, *Feature Engineering for the Win,* will be your guide to mastering this art. We'll explore why feature engineering is the secret weapon of successful data science projects, how it can elevate your models from mediocre to masterful, and equip you with a comprehensive toolbox of techniques to unlock the true potential of your data. From feature creation and transformation to selection and dimensionality reduction, you'll learn how to craft informative features that empower your models to achieve peak performance. So, get ready to transform your data from good to great and watch your machine learning models soar.

Feature engineering is the art of transforming this data into the perfect fuel for your model. This opening chapter lays the groundwork for your journey, explaining why feature engineering is the secret sauce for successful machine learning projects. We'll explore the limitations raw data poses for algorithms, unpack the core concept of feature engineering, and unveil the dramatic impact well-designed features can have on your model's accuracy, efficiency, and ability to generalize to unseen data. Get ready to unlock the true potential of your machine learning endeavors by mastering the art of feature engineering.The boundaries of what's possible, the quality of data fed to these models remains paramount. While complex algorithms and architectures are impressive feats of engineering, even the most sophisticated model is only as good as the information it's trained on. This is where feature engineering comes in.

It's the art and science of transforming raw data into meaningful attributes, the building blocks that a machine learning model can understand and leverage to make predictions or classifications. By thoughtfully crafting features, we can significantly improve the performance of our models, unlocking their true potential. This book serves as a comprehensive guide to feature engineering, equipping you with the knowledge and techniques to transform your data from good to great, and empower your machine learning models to achieve peak performance.

Machine learning algorithms are powerful tools, but like any tool, their effectiveness depends heavily on the quality of the raw materials they work with. In the case of machine learning, that raw material is data. However, data in its natural state is often messy, unrefined, and difficult for algorithms to understand. This is where feature engineering steps in. It's the process of transforming raw data into meaningful features, essentially creating a clear and concise language that machine learning models can readily comprehend. By carefully crafting these features, we can significantly improve the accuracy, efficiency, and overall performance of our models. This book delves into the world of feature engineering, providing you with the knowledge and techniques to unlock the true potential of your data and build powerful machine learning models.

## CHAPTER TWO

THE FOUNDATION OF FEATURE ENGINEERING

The foundation of any successful machine learning project is built upon strong data. But data, in its raw form, is often like a pile of unhewn stones – full of potential, but unusable in its current state. Feature engineering is the art and science of transforming this raw data into meticulously crafted building blocks, ready to be assembled into a powerful machine learning model. This first part of the book, "The Foundations of Feature Engineering," lays the groundwork for your journey. We'll explore the fundamental concepts: why raw data presents challenges for algorithms, what feature engineering truly is, and how it dramatically impacts the performance of your models. By understanding these core principles, you'll gain the essential knowledge to transform your data from a jumbled mess into the cornerstone of successful machine learning projects. The realm of machine learning is abuzz with innovation. Algorithms are constantly evolving, pushing the boundaries of what's possible in areas like image recognition, natural language processing, and intelligent automation. But amidst this technological marvel, there's a fundamental truth that often gets overlooked: the quality of data used to train these models is paramount.

Imagine a chef preparing a culinary masterpiece. Just throwing random ingredients into a pot won't result in a delectable dish. The quality and preparation of those ingredients are just as crucial as the recipe itself. In the world of machine learning, data serves as the "ingredients" for our models. But unlike neatly chopped vegetables and perfectly seasoned meats, raw data is often messy, unrefined, and difficult for algorithms to understand. This is where the art of feature engineering comes in. Think of feature engineering as the meticulous process of preparing your data for optimal performance in a machine learning model. It's the bridge that connects the raw, unprocessed information to the algorithms that can learn from it. Just as a chef transforms ingredients into a format that enhances the final dish, feature engineering transforms data into a format that empowers machine learning models to make accurate predictions or classifications.

FEATURE ENGINEERING MATTERS

In the thrilling world of machine learning, where algorithms churn through mountains of data, the quality of that data reigns supreme. Imagine feeding a state-of-the-art image recognition model a blurry, unlabeled picture it would struggle to identify even the most basic shapes. That's the crux of why feature engineering matters. It's the meticulous process of transforming raw data from this blurry mess into a crystal-clear picture, ready for a machine learning model to interpret and learn from.

Feature engineering is crucial for building powerful models:

- **Unlocking Hidden Potential:** Raw data often contains valuable insights buried beneath layers of noise and inconsistencies. Feature engineering helps extract these hidden gems by transforming the data into a format that highlights the relevant patterns and relationships for the model to grasp.
- **Speaking the Model's Language:** Machine learning models thrive on clear, concise information. Feature engineering acts as a translator, converting the raw data into a language the model can understand. This allows the model to learn more effectively and make more accurate predictions.
- **Boosting Model Performance:** Well-crafted features can significantly improve the accuracy, efficiency, and

generalizability of your models. By providing the model with the right information, you can significantly reduce errors and ensure your models perform optimally on unseen data.

- In essence, feature engineering is the bridge between your data and the powerful algorithms that can unlock its true potential. By investing time and effort into this crucial step, empower your machine learning models to soar to new heights of performance.

THE BOTTLENECK OF MACHINE LEARNING

A marvel of engineering, designed for peak performance. Now, picture fueling it with low-grade gasoline. While the engine itself is capable of incredible feats, the poor quality fuel hinders its ability to reach its full potential. This analogy perfectly illustrates the bottleneck of raw data in machine learning.

Raw data acts as a bottleneck for machine learning algorithms:

Complexity and Noise: Real-world data is inherently complex and noisy. It may contain missing values, inconsistencies, and irrelevant information. These factors make it difficult for algorithms to identify the underlying patterns and relationships crucial for accurate predictions.

The Curse of Dimensionality: High-dimensional data, with many features, can overwhelm machine learning algorithms. This "curse of dimensionality" leads to increased training time, computational complexity, and ultimately, hinders the model's ability to learn effectively.

Misinterpretation and Bias: Raw data can often contain hidden biases or reflect inherent real-world biases. These biases, if not addressed, can lead the model to learn incorrect or misleading patterns, impacting its overall performance and generalizability.

Think of a machine learning model as a student trying to learn a new language. Raw data, in its unprocessed form, is like a jumbled mess of words and phrases. Without proper grammar, structure, and context, it's incredibly difficult for the student (the model) to understand the true meaning and make sense of the information.

The Impact on Model Performance:

The consequences of neglecting feature engineering are severe:

- Reduced Accuracy: Raw data can lead to models that make inaccurate predictions or classifications.
- Overfitting and Underfitting: Without proper feature engineering, models can become overly reliant on specific features in the training data, leading to overfitting (poor performance on unseen data). Alternatively, they might underfit, failing to capture the relevant patterns altogether.
- Increased Training Time: Complex, unprocessed data requires more computational resources and time to train, hindering efficiency.

By addressing the bottleneck of raw data through feature engineering, we unlock the true potential of machine learning algorithms. Just like transforming low-grade fuel into high-octane gasoline allows the race car to perform at its best, feature engineering empowers machine learning models to achieve peak accuracy, efficiency, and generalizability.

## CHAPTER THREE

THE IMAPCT OF FEATURE ENGINEERING ON MODEL PERFORMANCE

In the realm of machine learning, where algorithms are constantly pushing the boundaries of what's possible, the quality of data remains the lifeblood of success. But just like a powerful engine sputters with low-grade fuel, even the most sophisticated algorithm struggles to learn effectively from raw, unprocessed data. This is where feature engineering steps in, acting as the invisible hand that dramatically transforms the impact of your models.

Raw data often resembles a treasure chest brimming with valuable insights, but buried beneath layers of noise and inconsistencies. Feature engineering acts as the key, unlocking these hidden gems. Through techniques like scaling, normalization, and encoding, it transforms data into a format that highlights the relevant patterns and relationships for the model to grasp. Imagine feeding a model a picture of a house. In its raw form, the image might be a jumble of pixels. Feature engineering can extract features like the number of windows, roof type, and overall size, creating a clear picture the model can understand and use to predict house prices accurately.

Speaking the Model's Language:

Machine learning models are like students eager to learn, but they require clear and concise instructions. Feature engineering acts as a translator, converting the raw data into a language the model can comprehend. This can involve techniques like creating interaction features by combining existing ones, or feature selection to choose the most informative features for the specific task. By presenting the model with well-defined features, you empower it to learn more effectively and make more accurate predictions.

Boosting Efficiency and Generalizability:

The impact of feature engineering extends beyond just accuracy. Well-crafted features can significantly improve the efficiency and generalizability of your models. Here's how:

- Reduced Training Time: By providing the model with the right information from the start, you can significantly reduce the time and computational resources needed for training. Imagine a student trying to learn a new language. If they have clear vocabulary and grammar, they'll learn much faster than if they're presented with a jumbled mess of words.

- Enhanced Generalizability: Feature engineering can help models perform well on unseen data, not just the data they were trained on. By focusing on extracting the underlying patterns and relationships within the data, rather than just memorizing specific features in the training set, the model is better equipped to handle new situations.

A Real-World Example:

Imagine you're building a model to predict customer churn (the likelihood of a customer leaving your service). Raw data might include customer demographics, purchase history, and support tickets. Feature engineering could involve creating features like "average monthly spend," "number of support tickets in the last year," or a new feature indicating "high-value customer" based on a combination of factors. By providing these informative features, you empower the model to identify patterns that predict churn risk more accurately, allowing you to take proactive steps to retain valuable customers.

Feature engineering is not a magic bullet, but it's a critical step in the machine learning workflow. By understanding the impact it has on model performance – improved accuracy, efficiency, and generalizability – you'll be well on your way to building models that deliver exceptional results. The next time you approach a machine learning project, remember: it's not just about the algorithm, but about the quality of the fuel you feed it. By investing time and effort in feature engineering, you can unlock the true potential of your data and propel your machine learning models to new heights of performance.

## CHAPTER FOUR

EXPLORATORY DATA ANALYSIS (EDA) FOR FEATURE ENGINEERING

Before embarking on the journey of crafting powerful features, we need to delve into the treasure trove of raw data itself. This is where Exploratory Data Analysis (EDA) steps in, acting as the essential first step for successful feature engineering. It's akin to an explorer charting a new territory; uncovering the landscape, identifying landmarks, and understanding the lay of the land before embarking on the feature engineering expedition. Through EDA, we gain a deep understanding of our data, its characteristics, potential pitfalls, and hidden gems. This knowledge becomes the foundation for creating features that are not only relevant, but also effective in empowering our machine learning models.

EDA serves as a springboard for feature engineering by:

Unveiling Data Distribution: EDA helps us visualize and understand the distribution of our data. Are there outliers? Are certain features skewed? This knowledge informs feature scaling and normalization techniques, ensuring all features are on a level playing field for the model.

Identifying Relationships: By analyzing relationships between features and the target variable, we can uncover hidden patterns and correlations. This paves the way for creating informative interaction features that capture complex relationships the model can leverage for better predictions.

Discovering Feature Biases and Issues: EDA helps us identify potential biases or inconsistencies within the data. Missing values, irrelevant features, and data quality issues can all be unearthed and addressed during EDA, leading to cleaner, more reliable features for our models.

By undertaking a thorough EDA, we gain invaluable insights into the strengths and weaknesses of our data. This knowledge empowers us to make informed decisions during feature engineering, ultimately leading to the creation of features that unlock the true potential of our machine learning models.

UNDERSTANDING YOUR DATA

In the captivating world of machine learning, where algorithms weave magic with data, the quality of that data reigns supreme. Before we delve into the art of feature engineering, meticulously crafting the building blocks for our models, we must first embark on a crucial journey: understanding our data. This foundational step is akin to a skilled architect meticulously analyzing the land before crafting a magnificent building. Just as a firm foundation is essential for a sturdy structure, a comprehensive understanding of your data is the bedrock of successful feature engineering.

Imagine feeding a complex image recognition model a blurry, unlabeled picture. It would struggle to identify even the most basic shapes. This exemplifies why understanding your data is paramount. Raw data, in its natural state, can be a labyrinth – a complex maze of information brimming with potential, but often riddled with inconsistencies, noise, and hidden patterns. By embarking on a thorough data exploration process, we transform this labyrinth into a well-lit pathway, ready for the feature engineering journey.

Understanding your data is the cornerstone of feature engineering: Through techniques like data visualization and statistical analysis, we gain valuable insights into the distribution of our data. Are there outliers lurking in the shadows, skewing the overall picture? Is a particular feature heavily skewed towards one end of the spectrum? By understanding these characteristics, we can identify potential issues and take corrective measures during feature engineering. Techniques like scaling and normalization come into play here, ensuring all features are on a level playing field for the machine learning model.

Data often holds hidden treasures – valuable patterns and relationships waiting to be unearthed. Through careful exploration, we can uncover these gems, the correlations and dependencies between features. This knowledge becomes the foundation for crafting powerful interaction features. Imagine building a model to predict house prices. Understanding the relationships between features like square footage, number of bedrooms, and location becomes crucial. By creating interaction features that capture these relationships (e.g., "price per square foot"), we empower the model to learn more effectively and make more accurate predictions.

Real-world data is rarely perfect. It can be riddled with biases, inconsistencies, and missing values. These issues, if left unaddressed, can lead to inaccurate and misleading feature engineering. By understanding these issues during data exploration, we can take proactive steps during feature engineering. Missing values can be imputed, irrelevant features can be removed, and potential biases can be mitigated through strategic feature selection techniques.

Benefits of Understanding Your Data:

By investing time and effort into understanding your data, you reap several benefits when it comes to feature engineering:

- Enhanced Feature Relevance: Features created with a deep understanding of the data are more likely to be relevant to the task at hand. This leads to models that focus on the information that truly matters, improving their overall performance.
- Reduced Training Time and Increased Efficiency: Feature engineering based on a solid understanding of the data can be more targeted and efficient. Irrelevant features are eliminated,

leading to cleaner data sets and reduced training times for your models.

- Improved Model Generalizability: By understanding the underlying patterns and relationships within the data, rather than just memorizing specific features, you can create features that generalize well to unseen data. This ensures your models perform well in real-world scenarios, not just on the training data they were exposed to.

Understanding your data is not just a preliminary step; it's an ongoing conversation throughout the machine learning workflow. By continuously analyzing and exploring your data, you gain valuable insights that inform your feature engineering decisions. This, in turn, leads to the creation of features that unlock the true potential of your machine learning models. Remember, a model is only as good as the data it's trained on. By taking the time to truly understand your data, you lay the foundation for building powerful and successful machine learning models.

PYTHON LIBRARIES

Python offers a rich ecosystem of libraries that are invaluable for feature engineering. Here's a breakdown of some of the most commonly used ones:

NumPy

The Backbone of Numerical Computations

NumPy is the cornerstone of numerical computing in Python. Its core data structure, the NumPy array, is a versatile and efficient tool for handling large datasets. Here's why it's essential for feature engineering:

High-performance array operations:

- NumPy arrays are optimized for numerical operations, offering significant speed advantages over Python lists. This efficiency is crucial when dealing with large datasets, which are common in machine learning.

- Array manipulation: NumPy provides a rich set of functions for creating, indexing, slicing, reshaping, and manipulating arrays. These operations are fundamental to feature engineering tasks like data cleaning, normalization, and transformation.
- Linear algebra: NumPy integrates seamlessly with linear algebra libraries, making it suitable for complex mathematical operations often required in feature engineering, such as matrix calculations and eigenvalue decomposition.
- Compatibility: NumPy arrays are compatible with many other scientific Python libraries, ensuring smooth integration into the data science workflow.

In essence, NumPy provides the foundation for numerical computations in Python, making it an indispensable tool for any data scientist involved in feature engineering.NumPy is the fundamental package for scientific computing in Python. It provides high-performance multi-dimensional array objects, along with tools for working with these arrays. Its efficiency in numerical operations makes it essential for handling large datasets and performing complex mathematical calculations.

Pandas

Built on top of NumPy, Pandas provides high-level data structures and manipulation tools. DataFrames, its primary data structure, offer a tabular representation of data, making it easy to handle and analyze diverse datasets. Pandas excels in data cleaning, exploration, and preparation, making it an indispensable tool for feature engineering.Pandas is a Python library built on top of NumPy, providing high-level data structures and manipulation tools designed for working with structured data. Its core data structures, Series and DataFrame, offer flexibility and efficiency in handling diverse datasets.

Key Features for Feature Engineering

- **Data ingestion:** Pandas can read data from various file formats (CSV, Excel, JSON, etc.) and databases, making it a versatile tool for data acquisition.

- **Data cleaning:** Handling missing values, outliers, and inconsistencies is streamlined with Pandas functions like fillna, dropna, and replace.
- **Data exploration:** Functions like describe, head, tail, and value_counts provide insights into data distribution and identify potential issues.
- **Data manipulation:** Pandas offers powerful tools for filtering, sorting, grouping, merging, and reshaping data, enabling the creation of new features and datasets.
- **Time series analysis:** Handling time-indexed data is a strength of Pandas, making it suitable for time-series feature engineering.

Pandas with NumPy's computational efficiency, data scientists can effectively explore, clean, and transform data into a suitable format for machine learning models.

Demonstrating Pandas for Feature Engineering

Loading and Exploring Data

```
import pandas as pd
import numpy as np
# Sample data (replace with your actual data)
data = {'Age': [25, 30, 35, 40],
'Income': [50000, 60000, 70000, 80000],
'City': ['New York', 'Los Angeles', 'Chicago', 'Houston']}
df = pd.DataFrame(data)
print(df.head())
print(df.describe())
```

Handling Missing Values

```
# Assuming some missing values
df['Income'].fillna(df['Income'].mean(), inplace=True)
```

Creating New Features

```
df['Age_squared'] = df['Age'] ** 2
df['Income_category'] = pd.cut(df['Income'], bins=[0, 50000, 75000, np.inf], labels=['Low', 'Medium', 'High'])
```

Data Transformation

```
from sklearn.preprocessing import StandardScaler
scaler = StandardScaler()
df[['Age', 'Income']] = scaler.fit_transform(df[['Age', 'Income']])
```

Data Aggregation

```
grouped_data = df.groupby('City').mean()
```

Feature Selection (Basic)

```
import matplotlib.pyplot as plt
import seaborn as sns
# Correlation matrix
corr_matrix = df.corr()
sns.heatmap(corr_matrix, annot=True)
plt.show()
```

Remember, real-world datasets often require more complex transformations and feature creation. Pandas provides a solid foundation for these tasks, but it's often combined with other libraries like NumPy and Scikit-learn for more advanced feature engineering.

Scikit-learn

Scikit-learn is a machine learning library that also offers robust feature engineering capabilities. It provides tools for preprocessing, feature selection, dimensionality reduction, and model evaluation. Its integration with other scientific Python libraries makes it a versatile choice for end-to-end machine learning projects.

is a powerful Python library that provides a comprehensive set of tools for machine learning, including preprocessing, feature selection, dimensionality reduction, and model evaluation. It's designed to interoperate seamlessly with NumPy and Pandas, making it a popular choice for data scientists.

Key Features for Feature Engineering

- **Preprocessing:** Offers functions for handling missing values, scaling features, encoding categorical variables, and more.
- **Feature selection:** Provides methods like univariate selection, recursive feature elimination, and embedded methods to

identify important features.

- **Dimensionality reduction:** Includes techniques like Principal Component Analysis (PCA), t-SNE, and feature extraction methods.
- **Model evaluation:** Offers metrics and cross-validation tools to assess feature engineering effectiveness.

Scikit-learn's user-friendly interface and extensive documentation make it accessible to both beginners and experienced practitioners. Its integration with other Python libraries ensures a smooth workflow for data analysis and model building.

Advanced Feature Engineering with Scikit-learn

Text Data Feature Extraction

```
from sklearn.feature_extraction.text import TfidfVectorizer
# Sample text data
corpus = [
'This is the first document.',
'This is the second second document.',
'And the third one, too.'
]
vectorizer = TfidfVectorizer()
X = vectorizer.fit_transform(corpus)
print(X.toarray())
```

Image Data Feature Extraction (Using scikit-image)

```
from skimage import feature
import numpy as np
# Assuming you have an image as a NumPy array
# Extract HOG features
hog_features = feature.hog(image, orientations=8,
pixels_per_cell=(16, 16),
cells_per_block=(2, 2), block_norm='L2')
```

Custom Transformers

```
Python
from sklearn.base import BaseEstimator, TransformerMixin
```

```
class CustomTransformer(BaseEstimator, TransformerMixin):
def __init__(self,
parameter1, parameter2):
self.parameter1 = parameter1
self.parameter2 = parameter2
def fit(self, X, y=None):
# Learn some parameters from the data
return self
def transform(self, X):
# Apply the learned parameters to transform the data
return transformed_data
```

Pipeline for Feature Engineering and Model Building

```
from sklearn.pipeline import Pipeline
from sklearn.svm import SVC
# Create a pipeline
pipeline = Pipeline([
('scaler', StandardScaler()),
('clf', SVC())
])
# Fit the pipeline to your data
pipeline.fit(X_train, y_train)
```

These examples showcase the versatility of Scikit-learn for various feature engineering tasks. Remember to adapt these techniques based on your specific dataset and problem.

Featuretools

Designed specifically for feature engineering, Featuretools automates the creation of features from complex datasets. It excels at handling relational data and automatically generates a vast feature space. Featuretools can significantly accelerate the feature engineering process, especially when dealing with large and intricate datasets.Featuretools is a powerful Python library specifically designed to automate the creation of features from complex datasets. It excels at handling relational data, where information is spread across multiple tables.

Key Features and Benefits

- **Deep Feature Synthesis (DFS):** Featuretools employs DFS to recursively explore relationships between entities and generate a vast feature space. This includes aggregations, transformations, and combinations of features.
- **EntitySets:** This data structure represents a collection of tables and their relationships, providing a structured way to define the data for feature engineering.
- **Feature Primitives:** Pre-defined functions for creating features, such as aggregations, transformations, and statistical calculations.
- **Scalability:** Handles large datasets efficiently, making it suitable for real-world applications.
- **Time-based features:** Effectively handles time-indexed data and generates time-based features.

Let's consider a customer churn prediction problem. We have a dataset with information about customers, their subscriptions, and their interactions with a product.

Data Structure:

- **Customers:** customer_id, age, gender, city, etc.
- **Subscriptions:** customer_id, subscription_type, start_date, end_date, etc.
- **Interactions:** customer_id, timestamp, event_type (e.g., login, purchase, support_ticket), etc.

Using Featuretools, we can:

1. **Define entities and relationships:** Create EntitySets to represent customers, subscriptions, and interactions.
2. **Specify feature primitives:** Define aggregations, transformations, and other functions to create features.
3. **Generate features:** Use Featuretools to automatically create features based on the defined entitysets and primitives.

Example features:

- **Customer-level features:**

    ◦ Total number of subscriptions
    ◦ Average subscription duration
    ◦ Recent purchase amount
    ◦ Number of support tickets in the last month

- **Subscription-level features:**

    ◦ Subscription churn rate
    ◦ Average revenue per user (ARPU)
    ◦ Subscription upgrade rate

By leveraging Featuretools, we can quickly generate a rich set of features without manually crafting them. These features can then be used to train a machine learning model to predict customer churn.

Limitations of Featuretools

While Featuretools is a powerful tool, it's essential to be aware of its limitations:

- **Computational cost:** Generating a vast feature space can be computationally expensive, especially for large datasets.
- **Feature relevance:** Not all generated features might be relevant to the prediction task, requiring feature selection.
- **Domain knowledge:** Understanding the domain is crucial for interpreting and selecting the most informative features.
- **Complex relationships:** For extremely complex datasets with many entities and relationships, Featuretools might struggle to capture all relevant interactions.

By understanding these limitations and combining Featuretools with domain expertise, data scientists can effectively leverage its capabilities for feature engineering. By automating the feature engineering process, Featuretools significantly reduces the time and effort required to create informative features. This allows data scientists to focus on higher-level tasks and explore a broader range of feature combinations. By effectively utilizing these libraries, data scientists can streamline the feature engineering process, improve data quality, and enhance the performance of their machine learning models.

Examples of Feature Engineering with Scikit-learn
Handling Categorical Data
One-hot encoding:
```python
from sklearn.preprocessing import OneHotEncoder
data = [['red'], ['blue'], ['green']]
encoder = OneHotEncoder()
encoded_data = encoder.fit_transform(data)
print(encoded_data.toarray())
```
Ordinal encoding:
```python
from sklearn.preprocessing import OrdinalEncoder
data = [['low'], ['medium'], ['high']]
encoder = OrdinalEncoder()
encoded_data = encoder.fit_transform(data)
print(encoded_data)
```
Scaling Numerical Features
Standardization:
```python
from sklearn.preprocessing import StandardScaler
data = [[0, 1], [1, 0], [2, 2]]
scaler = StandardScaler()
scaled_data = scaler.fit_transform(data)
print(scaled_data)
```
Normalization:
```python
from sklearn.preprocessing import MinMaxScaler
data = [[0, 1], [1, 0], [2, 2]]
scaler = MinMaxScaler()
scaled_data = scaler.fit_transform(data)
print(scaled_data)
```

Feature Selection

SelectKBest:

```
from sklearn.feature_selection import SelectKBest
from sklearn.feature_selection import chi2
X, y = load_iris(return_X_y=True)
selector = SelectKBest(chi2, k=2)
X_new = selector.fit_transform(X, y)
print(X_new.shape)
```

Polynomial Features

```
from sklearn.preprocessing import PolynomialFeatures
data = [[1, 2], [3, 4]]
poly = PolynomialFeatures(degree=2)
transformed_data = poly.fit_transform(data)
print(transformed_data)
```

These examples provide a basic overview of some common feature engineering tasks using Scikit-learn. It's essential to adapt these techniques based on the specific dataset and problem at hand.

IDENTIFYING DATA ISSUES AND BIASES

In the world of machine learning, data is the lifeblood of success. But just like a pristine diamond can be marred by hidden flaws, even seemingly clean data can harbor issues and biases. These impurities, if left unaddressed during feature engineering, can lead to inaccurate models and misleading results. This chapter delves into the critical task of identifying data issues and biases, equipping you to build a solid foundation for crafting powerful features.

Data Issues:

Data issues are like thorns on a beautiful rose – they can hinder the quality of your data and ultimately, the effectiveness of your features. Here are some common data issues to watch out for:

Missing Values: Missing data points can be a real headache. They can skew the distribution of features and introduce noise into your models. Techniques like imputation (filling in missing values) or feature deletion might be necessary during feature engineering to address this issue.

Inconsistent Data: Inconsistencies can arise from various sources, such as typos or different data formats. These inconsistencies can make it difficult for models to learn effectively. Techniques like data cleaning and standardization are crucial during feature engineering to ensure consistency across your data.

Outliers: Outliers are data points that fall far outside the typical range of values for a feature. While they can sometimes be indicative of valuable insights, they can also distort the overall distribution and mislead models. During feature engineering, you might need to decide whether to handle outliers through capping, winsorizing (replacing extreme values with a specific percentile), or removal depending on the context.

Data Biases:

Data biases are like a skewed lens, distorting the way we see the world and potentially leading to unfair or inaccurate results in our models. Here are some types of data biases to be aware of:

Selection Bias: This occurs when the data collection process is not random, leading to a sample that is not representative of the entire population. Imagine building a model to predict loan defaults using data only from customers with a history of on-time payments. This would likely lead to a biased model that underestimates the risk of defaults. During feature engineering, you might need to employ techniques like oversampling or undersampling to balance the data and mitigate selection bias.

Sampling Bias: This occurs when the data collection process favors certain types of data points over others. For example, a social media sentiment analysis model trained primarily on positive tweets would be biased towards positive sentiment. Feature engineering might involve techniques like data augmentation to introduce a wider variety of data points and lessen sampling bias.

Measurement Bias: This occurs when the way data is collected introduces inherent bias. Imagine using customer satisfaction surveys with poorly worded questions. During feature engineering, you might need to consider alternative data sources or refine the way data is collected to address measurement bias.

The Impact on Feature Engineering:

Data issues and biases, if left unchecked, can have a detrimental impact on feature engineering:

- Irrelevant Features: Feature engineering based on biased or inconsistent data can lead to the creation of irrelevant features that don't capture the true relationships within the data. This can hinder the performance of your models.
- Misleading Models: Models trained on features derived from biased data will inherit those biases and produce misleading results. Imagine a loan approval model trained on data with a gender bias. This could lead to unfair loan denials for qualified applicants.

Strategies for Mitigating Issues and Biases:

Here are some strategies to employ during feature engineering to mitigate data issues and biases:

- Data Cleaning and Preprocessing: Techniques like data cleaning, normalization, and outlier handling can address many common data issues and improve the overall quality of your data.
- Feature Selection and Transformation: By carefully selecting features that are relevant and unbiased, and using techniques like scaling and encoding, you can mitigate the impact of biases on your models.
- Domain Expertise and Exploratory Data Analysis (EDA): Leveraging your domain knowledge and conducting thorough EDA can help you identify potential biases and data issues early on in the process.

Identifying data issues and biases is a crucial step in the feature engineering workflow. By addressing these challenges proactively, you can build a solid foundation for crafting powerful features that empower your machine learning models to deliver accurate and unbiased results. Remember, the quality of your features is directly linked to the quality of your data. By taking the time to identify and address data issues and biases, you'll be well on your way to building exceptional machine learning models.

THE BROADER MLOps PIPELINE TECHNIQUE

MLOps encompasses the entire lifecycle of a machine learning model, from development to production and beyond. A core component of this is the MLOps pipeline, which typically includes the following key stages:

Continuous Integration and Continuous Delivery (CI/CD): This practice automates the building, testing, and deployment of machine learning models. Similar to traditional software development, CI/CD ensures code quality, consistency, and rapid deployment of model updates. However, in ML, it also includes testing data quality, model performance, and reproducibility. CI/CD is a fundamental practice in MLOps that automates the building, testing, and deployment of machine learning models. While it shares similarities with traditional software development CI/CD, it incorporates unique challenges and considerations specific to ML.

Key Components of MLOps CI/CD

- **Version control:** Managing code, data, and model versions is crucial for reproducibility and collaboration.
- **Automated testing:** This includes unit tests for code, integration tests for components, and model evaluation tests to assess performance metrics.
- **Data validation:** Ensuring data quality, consistency, and schema compliance is essential for model reliability.
- **Model training and evaluation:** Automating the training and evaluation process on different datasets and hyperparameters.
- **Deployment pipelines:** Defining and automating the process of deploying models to various environments (development, staging, production).
- **Infrastructure management:** Provisioning and managing the necessary compute resources for model training and deployment.

By implementing CI/CD, organizations can accelerate model development, improve quality, and reduce time-to-market. It also fosters collaboration between data scientists and engineers, enabling faster iteration and experimentation.

Model Deployment: This stage involves integrating the trained model into a production environment where it can be used to make predictions on new data. This often includes deploying the model as a web service or API, allowing other applications to consume its outputs. Model deployment is the crucial stage where a trained machine learning model transitions from a development environment to a production setting. It involves integrating the model into a live system where it can process new data and generate predictions or recommendations.

Key aspects of model deployment include:

- **Model serving:** Packaging the model into a format suitable for deployment, such as a serialized file or a containerized application.
- **Infrastructure selection:** Choosing the appropriate deployment environment, whether it's a cloud platform, on-premises servers, or edge devices.
- **API creation:** Developing APIs to expose the model's capabilities to other applications or systems.
- **Scalability:** Ensuring the deployment can handle varying workloads and traffic.
- **Monitoring and logging:** Continuously tracking model performance, resource utilization, and error rates.

Successful model deployment requires careful consideration of factors like latency, throughput, cost, and security. It often involves collaboration between data scientists, engineers, and DevOps teams.

Model Monitoring: Once a model is in production, it's crucial to continuously monitor its performance. This includes tracking key metrics, detecting concept drift (changes in data distribution), and identifying potential issues. Monitoring also involves model retraining or redeployment as needed to maintain performance. Model monitoring is an essential component of MLOps that ensures the ongoing health and performance of a deployed model. It involves continuously tracking and analyzing various aspects of the model's behavior in production.

Key elements of model monitoring include:

- **Performance metrics:** Tracking key performance indicators (KPIs) to assess the model's accuracy, precision, recall, or other relevant metrics. Any significant deviation from established baselines can indicate performance degradation.
- **Data drift:** Detecting changes in the distribution of input data compared to the training data. Data drift can significantly impact model performance and requires timely intervention.
- **Concept drift:** Identifying changes in the underlying relationship between input data and target variable. This is a more subtle form of drift that can be challenging to detect but has significant implications for model accuracy.
- **Model explainability:** Monitoring model explanations over time can help identify changes in feature importance or model behavior that might indicate issues.
- **Alerting:** Setting up alerts for critical events, such as performance drops, data drift, or system failures, to enable timely response.

By establishing a robust model monitoring system, organizations can proactively identify and address issues, ensuring that models continue to deliver value over time.

MLOps creates a streamlined and efficient process for developing, deploying, and maintaining machine learning models. This approach helps organizations to rapidly iterate on models, improve their performance, and ensure that they are delivering value to the business.

FEATURE VISUALIZATION TECHNIQUES

Feature engineering acts as the sculptor, transforming raw data into the building blocks that empower our models. But how do we, the engineers, truly understand the impact of these features on the model's decision-making process? This is where feature visualization techniques step in, acting as a powerful lens that allows us to peer into the inner workings of our models and gain invaluable insights into the role each feature plays.

By visualizing features, we can not only assess their effectiveness but also refine our feature engineering strategies and ensure our models are learning from the information that truly matters. Here's a deeper dive into some key feature visualization techniques:

1. Feature Importance:

Understanding the Hierarchy: Feature importance techniques quantify the contribution of each feature to the model's predictions. This allows us to identify the most influential features, the ones that have the greatest impact on the model's output. Techniques like permutation importance or feature selection algorithms can be used.

Prioritizing Feature Engineering Efforts: By understanding which features are most important, we can prioritize our feature engineering efforts. We can focus on refining and improving the most impactful features, ensuring the model learns from the most relevant information first.

2. Feature Distribution Visualization:

Unveiling the Data Landscape: Visualizing the distribution of features helps us understand the underlying patterns within our data. Techniques like histograms, boxplots, and density plots can be used.

Identifying Outliers and Skewness: These visualizations can reveal outliers, data points that fall far outside the typical range for a feature. They can also expose skewness, where the data is concentrated on one side of the distribution. Addressing these issues through feature engineering techniques like scaling or outlier handling can improve model performance.

3. Feature Interactions:

Exploring Synergies and Conflicts: Not all features work in isolation. Visualization techniques like scatter plots and pair plots can help us explore the interactions between features. These interactions can be synergistic, where features combined amplify their impact, or conflicting, where they work against each other.

Crafting Powerful Interaction Features: Feature engineering can leverage these insights to create new features that capture these interactions. For example, imagine building a model to predict customer churn. Visualizing the interaction between "purchase frequency" and "average order value" might reveal that customers with both high purchase frequency and high average order value are less likely to churn. A new interaction feature capturing this relationship could be created to improve model performance.

4. Saliency Maps and Grad-CAM:

Visualizing Feature Activation: These advanced techniques create visual heatmaps that highlight the regions of an input image (for computer vision tasks) or the specific words or phrases within a text input (for natural language processing tasks) that contribute most to the model's prediction.

Understanding Model Attention: By visualizing the areas the model focuses on, we can gain valuable insights into how it interprets the input data and which features it relies on most heavily. This can help us identify potential biases in the data or the model itself, and refine our feature engineering strategies accordingly.

Benefits of Feature Visualization:

- Improved Feature Engineering: By visualizing features, we can identify irrelevant features, assess the impact of feature engineering techniques, and ultimately create a more effective set of features for our models.
- Debugging Model Behavior: Feature visualization can help us diagnose issues with our models by identifying features that are not contributing meaningfully to the predictions. This allows us

to refine our feature engineering approach and improve model performance.

- Enhanced Communication and Explainability: Visualizations can be powerful tools for communicating the inner workings of a model to stakeholders. By showcasing how features contribute to predictions, we can build trust and understanding around the model's behavior.

Feature visualization techniques are not just a luxury; they're an essential part of the feature engineering workflow. By peering into the inner workings of our models, we gain a deeper understanding of how features are used and can make informed decisions to refine our feature engineering strategies. Remember, feature engineering is an iterative process, and visualization serves as a valuable feedback loop, guiding us towards creating features that empower our models to achieve exceptional performance.

## CHAPTER FIVE

FEATURES ENGINEERING TECHNIQUES

In the realm of machine learning, where algorithms are like sculptors shaping raw data into powerful models, feature engineering serves as the toolkit. It's the collection of techniques we employ to transform raw data into meaningful features, the building blocks that a machine learning model can understand and leverage to make accurate predictions or classifications. These techniques range from handling missing values and outliers to creating entirely new features by combining existing ones. By mastering this diverse toolbox of feature engineering techniques, we empower our models to learn from the right information, ultimately leading to superior performance and unlocking the true potential of our machine learning projects. A toolbox filled with techniques to transform raw data into meaningful features. These features become the building blocks that machine learning algorithms can understand and leverage to make accurate predictions or classifications. By exploring various feature engineering techniques, we can unlock the true potential of our data and empower our models to perform at their peak.

FEATURE CREATION AND TRANSFORMATION

In the captivating world of machine learning, where algorithms act as the engines that drive innovation, the fuel that powers them is data. But raw data, much like a lump of unrefined coal, holds its potential locked away. Feature creation and transformation, the cornerstones of feature engineering, are the crucial processes that unlock this potential. Imagine a sculptor transforming a rough block of stone into a masterpiece. Similarly, feature creation and transformation meticulously sculpt raw data into features – the building blocks that empower machine learning models. Through these techniques, we extract hidden patterns, unveil relationships within the data, and ultimately, craft features that speak a language the model can understand. By embarking on this journey of feature creation and transformation, we pave the way for the creation of powerful and effective machine learning models. Feature creation is like gathering materials you take the raw data you have and use it to construct new features that might be more informative for your model.

Deriving new features: You can use your domain knowledge or analyze data patterns to create new features.

For example, if you're predicting house prices, you could create a new feature by combining square footage and number of bedrooms.

Encoding categorical features: Some models struggle with text data. Feature creation techniques like one-hot encoding convert categorical variables (like "color") into numerical representations the model can understand.

Feature interaction: This involves multiplying existing features to capture potential relationships between them. Imagine features for income and years of experience. Their product might indicate earning potential.

Feature Transformation

Think of feature transformation as shaping your building materials. Here, you modify the existing features to make them more suitable for your machine learning model. Common goals include:

- Normalization: Scaling features to a common range can improve the performance of some algorithms. Imagine features in different units (inches and centimeters). Normalization ensures they contribute equally.

- Handling outliers: Extreme values can skew your model. Feature transformation techniques can address this by capping outliers or winsorizing (replacing them with values closer to the central tendency).
- Improving linearity: Some models work better with linear relationships. Transformations like log functions can make non-linear features more linear.

Feature creation and transformation are essential for building effective machine learning models. By carefully crafting features, you give your model the best possible chance to learn from your data and make accurate predictions. Imagine trying to build a house with mismatched, uneven bricks. Feature creation and transformation are like sorting and shaping your bricks to ensure a sturdy, well-built structure (machine learning model). Feature creation and transformation are iterative processes. You might need to experiment with different techniques to find what works best for your data and model.

There's a balance to be struck. Creating too many features can lead to overfitting, where the model memorizes the training data but performs poorly on unseen data.

These are data pre-processing techniques used in feature engineering to address the issue of features having different scales or units. This can lead to problems in machine learning algorithms, as features with larger magnitudes tend to dominate the learning process and overshadow features with smaller values. Scaling and normalization aim to create a level playing field for all features by transforming them to a common scale.

Feature Scaling

- Broadly refers to any technique that rescales the features of your data.
- The goal is to bring all features into a similar range.

- This doesn't necessarily change the distribution of the data itself.

Common Scaling Techniques:

Min-Max Scaling: Scales features to a range between 0 and 1 (or any specified minimum and maximum values). This is a simple and effective technique for many algorithms.

- Formula: $(x - min(X)) / (max(X) - min(X))$

Standardization: Scales features by subtracting the mean and then dividing by the standard deviation. This results in features with a mean of 0 and a standard deviation of 1. This technique is particularly useful for algorithms sensitive to Euclidean distances (like k-Nearest Neighbors).

- Formula: $(x - mean(X)) / std(X)$

Normalization

A specific type of scaling where the data is transformed to follow a specific distribution, typically a normal distribution (bell curve).

Normalization can be considered a more radical transformation than scaling, as it alters the shape of the data distribution.

Choosing the Right Technique

The choice between scaling and normalization, and the specific technique used, depends on the machine learning algorithm and the data itself. Here are some general guidelines:

- Use Min-Max scaling or standardization for algorithms that are sensitive to feature magnitudes (e.g., gradient descent, k-Nearest Neighbors).
- Use normalization for algorithms that assume a normal distribution (e.g., Principal Component Analysis).

Benefits of Feature Scaling and Normalization

- Improved Algorithm Performance: By ensuring all features contribute equally, scaling and normalization can lead to better convergence and accuracy of machine learning models.
- Fairer Feature Comparison: Different units or scales are put on a common ground, allowing for a more objective evaluation of feature importance.
- Faster Convergence: In gradient-based optimization algorithms, scaling can often speed up the learning process.

Remember:

- Scaling and normalization are essential steps in data pre-processing for machine learning.
- The choice of technique depends on the specific algorithm and data.

By understanding these techniques, you can effectively prepare your data for machine learning tasks and achieve better results.

ENCODING CATEGORICAL FEATURES

Categorical features, also known as nominal features, represent data that falls into distinct categories with no inherent order. Examples include shirt color (red, blue, green), customer type (bronze, silver, gold), or city names. However, most machine learning algorithms work best with numerical data. This is where encoding comes in.

Encoding is the process of transforming categorical features into a numerical representation that machine learning models can understand. Here are some common encoding techniques:

1. Label Encoding:

- Assigns a unique integer value to each category.
- Simple and computationally efficient.
- Doesn't capture any inherent order in the categories (e.g., red = 1, blue = 2 doesn't mean blue is "better" than red).

- May lead to issues with algorithms that assume a numerical relationship between categories.

2. One-Hot Encoding:

- Creates a new binary feature for each category.
- A data point is represented by a vector of 1s and 0s, where 1 indicates the presence of that category and 0 indicates its absence.
- Captures all information about the categories but can significantly increase the number of features, especially with a high number of categories.

3. Ordinal Encoding:

- Assigns numerical values to categories that reflect their inherent order (e.g., customer satisfaction: very dissatisfied = 1, dissatisfied = 2, neutral = 3, satisfied = 4, very satisfied = 5).
- Only useful if the categories have a natural ordering.
- Similar to label encoding in terms of computational efficiency.

4. Frequency Encoding (or Count Encoding):

- Assigns a numerical value to each category based on its frequency in the dataset.
- More frequent categories get higher values.
- Can be useful for capturing the importance of categories based on their prevalence.
- May not be suitable for all algorithms.

5. Target Encoding:

- Assigns a numerical value to each category based on the average target variable (e.g., average income) for data points belonging to that category.

- Can be powerful but leads to data leakage if used for both training and testing data (as it uses target information).
- Typically used as a technique for boosting model performance, but use with caution.

Choosing the Right Encoding Technique
The best encoding technique depends on several factors:

- Type of categorical feature: Nominal (no order) vs. ordinal (with order)
- Number of categories: One-hot encoding can become cumbersome with many categories.
- Machine learning algorithm: Some algorithms handle categorical features better than others.

Here are some general guidelines:

- Use label encoding or ordinal encoding for nominal or ordinal features with a small number of categories.
- Use one-hot encoding for nominal features with a moderate number of categories, but be aware of the increase in dimensionality.
- Consider frequency encoding or target encoding for specific scenarios, but be mindful of their limitations.

By understanding these techniques and choosing the most appropriate one for your data and model, you can effectively encode your categorical features and improve the performance of your machine learning projects.

FEATURE DISCRETIZATION AND BINNING

Machine learning algorithms often thrive on numerical data. But what about features that are continuous, like temperature, income, or customer age? These features hold valuable information, but feeding them directly into models can sometimes lead to issues. This is where feature discretization and its close cousin, binning, come into play.

Feature Discretization

Discretization is the process of transforming a continuous feature into a categorical feature. It essentially groups continuous values into a finite number of intervals, or "bins." This can be beneficial for several reasons:

- Improved Model Performance: Discretization can simplify complex relationships between features and the target variable, potentially leading to better model performance, especially for algorithms that struggle with continuous data.
- Reduced Computational Cost: By reducing the number of unique values, discretization can make training models faster and potentially reduce memory usage.
- Data Preprocessing for Specific Algorithms: Some algorithms, like decision trees, inherently work with categorical data. Discretization allows you to use such algorithms with continuous features.

Binning - A Discretization Technique

Binning is the most common method for feature discretization. It involves dividing the range of the continuous feature into a predefined number of bins (intervals). Each data point's original value is then replaced by the bin it falls into. Here are some common binning strategies:

- Equal-Width Binning: Creates bins with the same width across the entire range of the feature. This is simple but may not capture the underlying distribution of the data well, especially if the data is skewed.
- Equal-Frequency Binning: Divides the data into bins containing roughly the same number of data points. This ensures all bins are equally represented but can result in bins with varying widths.

- Percentile-Based Binning: Splits the data into percentiles (e.g., quartiles, deciles). This approach is useful when the data is skewed, as it ensures each bin captures a similar proportion of the data.

Choosing the Right Discretization Strategy

The optimal strategy depends on your data and the specific machine learning task. Here are some factors to consider:

- Data Distribution: If your data is skewed, equal-frequency binning or percentile-based binning might be better suited.
- Number of Bins: Too few bins can lead to information loss, while too many can increase complexity. Experiment with different binning options to find the sweet spot.
- Machine Learning Algorithm: Some algorithms may be more sensitive to the choice of binning strategy than others.

Beyond Basic Binning

While binning is a powerful tool, there are more advanced discretization techniques like:

- Chi-Squared Automatic Binning: Uses a statistical test to determine optimal bin boundaries based on the relationship between the feature and the target variable.
- Entropy-Based Discretization: Employs information entropy to create bins that minimize information loss.

Discretization can be a valuable data pre-processing step, but it's not a silver bullet. Evaluate its impact on your model performance. Experiment with different discretization strategies and binning techniques to find the best fit for your data and model.

CREATING INTERACTION FEATURES

In machine learning, models often learn from individual features, but real-world phenomena often involve complex relationships between features. Interaction features capture these relationships by combining existing features to create new ones that represent their joint effect on the target variable. This can significantly improve the performance of your model.

Understanding Interaction Effects

Imagine predicting house prices. While individual features like area and number of bedrooms are important, the interaction between them is crucial. A larger house with fewer bedrooms might not be as valuable as a smaller house with more bedrooms. Interaction features help capture such nuanced relationships.

Techniques for Creating Interaction Features

There are several ways to create interaction features:

Manual Feature Engineering: Based on domain knowledge, you can identify features that likely interact and create new features by multiplying, adding, or using more complex functions on them (e.g., area * number_of_bedrooms).

Polynomial Features: This technique automatically creates interaction features by raising existing features to specified powers (e.g., area^2, number_of_bedrooms^2, area * number_of_bedrooms). However, this can lead to a combinatorial explosion of features, especially with many initial features.

Tree-Based Models (Decision Trees, Random Forests): These models inherently capture interactions by splitting data based on combinations of features. You can leverage these models to identify important interactions and create new features based on those insights.

Benefits of Using Interaction Features

- Improved Model Performance: By capturing complex relationships, interaction features can significantly boost the accuracy and generalizability of your model.
- Better Model Interpretability: When interactions are explicit features, it's easier to understand how different features influence the target variable together.

Challenges and Considerations

- Curse of Dimensionality: Creating too many interaction features can lead to overfitting and hinder model performance. Choose interactions based on domain knowledge or feature importance analysis.
- Data Sparsity: With many interaction features, each combination might have few data points. This can be mitigated by using techniques like regularization or dimensionality reduction.

Choosing the Right Approach

The best method for creating interaction features depends on your data, the number of initial features, and your model type:

- **For smaller datasets and fewer features:** Manual feature engineering or polynomial features might be suitable.
- **For larger datasets or complex relationships:** Tree-based models can be a powerful choice to identify and leverage interactions.

Interaction features can significantly improve model performance and interpretability. Balance the benefits with the potential downsides like curse of dimensionality. Choose the creation method based on your data and model complexity.

WEBINARS AND WORKSHOPS FOR FEATURE ENGINEERING

Webinars and workshops on feature engineering offer invaluable opportunities for data scientists and practitioners to enhance their skills and stay updated on the latest trends. These interactive sessions provide a platform to learn from industry experts, network with peers, and gain hands-on experience. Topics typically cover a wide range of subjects, including feature selection, transformation, engineering for specific domains (like finance, healthcare, or marketing), and the integration of feature engineering into the broader machine learning pipeline. By attending these events, participants can acquire practical knowledge, troubleshoot challenges, and discover innovative approaches to feature engineering, ultimately improving the performance and interpretability of their models.

Beginner-Level Topics

Feature Engineering Fundamentals: Covering basic concepts, data types, and essential techniques.Feature engineering is the critical process of transforming raw data into meaningful features that can be effectively utilized by machine learning models. It involves understanding data types, handling missing values and outliers, and creating new features that capture relevant information. By mastering these foundational techniques, data scientists can lay the groundwork for building robust and accurate predictive models.

Exploratory Data Analysis (EDA) for Feature Discovery: How to extract insights from data to inform feature engineering.Exploratory Data Analysis (EDA) is a critical first step in the feature engineering process. By delving into the data, data scientists can uncover hidden patterns, identify relationships between variables, and detect anomalies. EDA involves a combination of statistical summaries and visual exploration to understand data distributions, correlations, and outliers. These insights are invaluable for selecting relevant features, creating new ones, and addressing data quality issues. Essentially, EDA serves as a foundation for informed feature engineering decisions, helping to maximize the predictive power of machine learning models.

Handling Missing Values and Outliers: Strategies for dealing with common data quality issues.Handling missing values and outliers is crucial for data quality and model performance. Missing values can distort statistical measures and lead to biased models if not addressed properly. Common strategies include imputation (replacing missing values with estimated values), deletion (removing rows or columns with missing data), or considering missingness as a feature. Outliers, which are data points significantly deviating from the norm, can distort statistical measures and reduce model accuracy. Techniques like z-score, interquartile range (IQR), and visual inspection can help identify outliers. Once identified, they can be removed, capped, or handled using robust statistical methods. Careful consideration of the dataset and the specific problem at hand is essential when choosing the appropriate approach for handling missing values and outliers.

Intermediate-Level Topics

- **Advanced Feature Engineering Techniques:** Exploring techniques like interaction features, polynomial features, and target encoding.
- **Feature Selection Methods:** In-depth discussion on filter, wrapper, and embedded methods.
- **Dimensionality Reduction Techniques:** Covering PCA, t-SNE, and other methods.

Advanced Topics

- **Feature Engineering for Time Series Data:** Addressing challenges and techniques for time-series data.
- **Feature Engineering for Text Data:** Exploring text preprocessing, representation, and feature extraction.
- **Automated Feature Engineering:** Discussing AutoML and its role in feature engineering.

Industry-Specific Topics

- **Feature Engineering for Healthcare:** Focusing on medical image analysis, patient data, and clinical trials.
- **Feature Engineering for Finance:** Covering fraud detection, risk assessment, and algorithmic trading.
- **Feature Engineering for Marketing:** Discussing customer segmentation, recommendation systems, and churn prediction.

FEATURE SELECTION AND DIMENSIONALITY REDUCTION

In the realm of machine learning, where data is king, the quality and relevance of features play a critical role in model success. However, datasets often contain a multitude of features, some highly informative and others potentially irrelevant or redundant. This can lead to several challenges. Features with vastly different scales can dominate the learning process, obscuring the contribution of less prominent but potentially valuable ones. Additionally, high-dimensional data can increase computational costs and make models prone to overfitting, where they learn the specifics of the training data but struggle to generalize to unseen examples. To navigate these issues and unlock the true potential of your data, two key techniques come into play: feature selection and dimensionality reduction. Feature selection acts as a curator, meticulously choosing the most informative features that best represent the underlying relationships within the data. This not only streamlines the learning process but also enhances model interpretability, allowing us to understand which features hold the most weight in influencing the target variable. Dimensionality reduction, on the other hand, takes a different approach. Instead of selecting specific features, it transforms the data into a lower-dimensional space while aiming to preserve the most important information. This not only reduces computational burden but can also lead to more robust models by mitigating the curse of dimensionality. By employing these techniques, we can transform our data from a cluttered mess into a lean and efficient representation, empowering machine learning models to make accurate predictions and uncover the hidden secrets within the data.

FEATURE SELECTION IMPORTANTS

Algorithms learn from data, the quality and relevance of features are paramount. But datasets often brim with features, some highly informative and others potentially irrelevant or redundant. This abundance of features can lead to several problems that feature selection helps address:

Improved Model Performance: Imagine training a model to predict customer churn. While a customer's age, income, and location are likely important, including their favorite color might not be. Irrelevant features can act like noise, confusing the model and hindering its ability to learn the true relationships between features and the target variable. Feature selection helps eliminate these distractions, allowing the model to focus on the most relevant information and ultimately leading to better predictions.

Reduced Overfitting: High-dimensional data, with a vast number of features, can lead to a phenomenon called overfitting. This occurs when a model memorizes the specific details of the training data but fails to generalize well to unseen examples. By selecting a smaller set of informative features, feature selection helps the model learn the underlying patterns in the data rather than just the quirks of the training set. This results in models that are more robust and perform better on new data.

Faster Training and Reduced Computational Cost: Training machine learning models can be computationally expensive, especially with high-dimensional data. Feature selection acts like a filter, reducing the number of features the model needs to process. This translates to faster training times and lower computational resources needed.

Enhanced Model Interpretability: When you have a complex model with numerous features, it can be challenging to understand which features are most influential in making predictions. Feature selection helps by identifying the key players, making the model's decision-making process more transparent and easier to interpret. This is crucial in domains where understanding the "why" behind a prediction is as important as the prediction itself.

Addressing the Curse of Dimensionality: As the number of features increases, the amount of data needed to train a model effectively grows exponentially. This phenomenon, known as the curse of dimensionality, can become a major obstacle in high-dimensional settings. Feature selection helps alleviate this curse by reducing the dimensionality of the data, allowing models to learn effectively even with limited data.

In essence, feature selection acts as a gatekeeper, ensuring that only the most relevant and informative features enter the machine learning model. This not only streamlines the learning process but also leads to models that are more accurate, efficient, and interpretable. By carefully selecting features, you can unlock the true potential of your data and empower your machine learning models to make better predictions.

FILTER METHODS FOR FEATURE SELECTION

In the realm of feature selection, filter methods stand as a powerful first line of defense against the curse of dimensionality. Unlike their counterparts, wrapper and embedded methods, which rely on involving the machine learning model itself in the selection process, filter methods operate independently. This makes them computationally efficient and agnostic to the specific learning algorithm you plan to use. Their core principle lies in evaluating each feature based on a statistical measure that reflects its relevance to the target variable. These measures can be as simple as correlation coefficients for continuous features, where a high correlation indicates a strong relationship between the feature and the target. For categorical features, chi-square tests or information gain can be used to assess the informativeness of a feature in discriminating between different target values.

Once each feature has a score based on its chosen metric, filter methods proceed with a selection strategy. This might involve setting a threshold and discarding features that fall below it, essentially creating a binary classification of relevant and irrelevant. Alternatively, you can choose a specific number of top-ranking features to retain. This approach ensures you capture the most informative features while keeping the dimensionality manageable. The beauty of filter methods lies in their simplicity and speed. They can quickly sift through a vast number of features, providing an initial shortlist of strong candidates for further analysis. However, it's important to remember that filter methods operate in isolation, making no attempt to consider feature interactions. This can sometimes lead them to overlook features that might be individually weak but become highly informative when combined with others. Additionally, the choice of statistical measure can impact the selection process. It's often recommended to experiment with different metrics and cutoffs to find the optimal configuration for your specific dataset and machine learning task. Nevertheless, filter methods remain a valuable tool in the feature selection toolbox, offering a fast and effective way to identify the most promising features and pave the way for further exploration with more intricate feature selection techniques.

In the machine learning domain, where data often explodes with features, feature selection becomes crucial. Filter methods offer a powerful approach to tackle this challenge. Here's a breakdown of their key characteristics:

Standalone approach:

Unlike wrapper and embedded methods that involve the machine learning model, filter methods operate independently.

Benefits:

- Computational Efficiency: They are lightning-fast, making them ideal for sifting through a large number of features.

- Algorithm Agnostic: They work for various machine learning algorithms, as they don't rely on the specific learning process.

Core Principle: Statistical Evaluation

Filter methods assess each feature individually based on a statistical measure. This measure reflects the feature's relevance to the target variable (what you're trying to predict).

Choosing the Right Measure:

Continuous Features: Correlation coefficients are popular choices. A high correlation indicates a strong relationship between the feature and the target.

Example: Correlation between income level and loan default rate.

Categorical Features: Chi-square tests or information gain come into play. These assess how well the feature helps distinguish between different target values.

Example: Chi-square test to see if shirt color (red, blue, green) is related to customer purchase decisions.

Feature Selection Strategies:

- Thresholding: Set a cut-off point. Features with scores below the threshold are discarded.
- Top-K Selection: Choose a specific number (K) of top-ranking features to retain. This ensures the most informative features are included while keeping dimensionality in check.

Advantages of Filter Methods:

- Speed and Efficiency: They quickly identify promising features, saving time and computational resources.
- Simplicity: Easy to understand and implement.

Limitations to Consider:

Feature Independence: Filter methods don't account for interactions between features. A feature might be weak on its own but become highly informative when combined with others. These interactions can be missed.

Measure Dependence: The choice of statistical measure can impact the selection process. Experimenting with different metrics is often recommended.

Overall, filter methods are a valuable asset in the feature selection arsenal. They provide a fast and effective way to identify the most relevant features, paving the way for further exploration with more intricate techniques. Filter methods are a great first step, but they shouldn't be the only step. Consider combining them with other feature selection techniques to create a robust and informative feature set for your machine learning models.

WRAPPER METHODS FOR FEATURE SELECTION

In the feature selection battlefield, where the fight against irrelevant features is waged, wrapper methods emerge as a powerful alternative to filter methods. Unlike their filter method counterparts, which operate independently, wrapper methods enlist the help of the machine learning model itself. This symbiotic relationship allows them to assess the impact of different feature subsets on the model's performance, ultimately selecting the combination that leads to the most accurate predictions. This approach offers a more targeted selection process, but with its own set of advantages and considerations to explore. Let's delve deeper into the fascinating world of wrapper methods and uncover their unique capabilities in the realm of feature selection.

In the feature selection arena, where identifying the most relevant features is key, wrapper methods offer a distinct approach compared to filter methods. Here's a breakdown of wrapper methods and their characteristics:

Wrapper Methods

Model-Centric Selection: Unlike filter methods, wrapper methods leverage the machine learning model itself during the selection process.

Symbiotic Relationship: They evaluate different combinations of features based on how well they improve the model's performance. This creates a feedback loop, where the model's performance guides feature selection.

Benefits of Wrapper Methods:

- Targeted Selection: By directly considering the impact on model performance, wrapper methods can identify feature combinations that are most beneficial for your specific learning task.
- Potential for Interaction Discovery: Because wrapper methods evaluate feature subsets, they can potentially discover synergistic relationships between features that filter methods might miss.

Challenges of Wrapper Methods:

- Computational Cost: Evaluating every possible combination of features can be computationally expensive, especially with a high number of features.
- Risk of Overfitting: Since the model is used in the selection process, there's a risk of overfitting to the training data. This can lead to models that perform well on the training data but poorly on unseen data.

Common Search Strategies:

- Forward Selection: Starts with an empty set of features and iteratively adds the feature that leads to the most significant improvement in model performance.
- Backward Elimination: Begins with all features and iteratively removes the feature that has the least negative impact on model performance.
- Bidirectional Elimination (Stepwise Selection): Combines forward selection and backward elimination, allowing for both adding and removing features.

Choosing the Right Wrapper Method:

The best strategy depends on the number of features and the computational resources available. Forward selection is a good starting point for large datasets, while backward elimination might be suitable for smaller datasets.

Overall, wrapper methods offer a powerful approach to feature selection by directly considering their impact on the machine learning model's performance. However, their computational cost and risk of overfitting need to be carefully considered.

Advanced Search Strategies:

Beyond the basic forward selection, backward elimination, and stepwise selection, there are more advanced search strategies used in wrapper methods:

Genetic Algorithms: Inspired by biological evolution, these algorithms mimic natural selection to iteratively improve feature subsets based on their performance.

Simulated Annealing: This technique uses a temperature parameter that allows for occasional exploration of less promising feature combinations, potentially leading to the discovery of unexpected but effective feature sets.

Addressing Overfitting:

Several techniques can help mitigate the risk of overfitting when using wrapper methods:

Cross-Validation: This involves splitting the data into training and validation sets. The feature selection process happens on the training set, and the final model's performance is evaluated on the unseen validation set. This helps ensure the selected features generalize well to new data.

Regularization Techniques: These techniques penalize models for having too many features, discouraging overfitting. L1 and L2 regularization are common examples.

Choosing the Right Method:

The best method for you depends on several factors:

- Number of Features: For a large number of features, wrapper methods can become computationally expensive. Consider filter methods as a first step in such cases.
- Model Complexity: If your model is prone to overfitting, filter methods might be a safer choice.
- Computational Resources: Wrapper methods require more computational power than filter methods.

Wrapper methods offer a powerful approach to feature selection, especially when you want to identify feature combinations that directly impact your model's performance. However, their computational cost and risk of overfitting need to be balanced with the benefits. By carefully considering these factors and employing techniques to mitigate overfitting, wrapper methods can be a valuable tool in your feature selection toolbox.

DIMENSIONALITY REDUCTION TECHNIQUES (PCA,LDA)

Machine learning, where data often resides in high-dimensional spaces, dimensionality reduction techniques play a critical role in empowering models. These techniques transform the data into a lower-dimensional space while aiming to preserve the most important information. Two prominent methods stand out: Principal Component Analysis (PCA) and Linear Discriminant Analysis (LDA). PCA acts as a versatile tool, uncovering the underlying structure of the data and identifying the directions of maximum variance. This allows for efficient compression without significant loss of information. LDA, on the other hand, takes a more targeted approach specifically suited for classification tasks. It maximizes the separation between different classes in the data, projecting the data onto a lower-dimensional space that best distinguishes between them. Both PCA and LDA offer valuable tools for dimensionality reduction, each catering to specific needs in the machine learning landscape.

In the world of machine learning, where data can sprawl across many dimensions, dimensionality reduction techniques emerge as heroes. These techniques transform complex, high-dimensional data into a lower-dimensional space, all while striving to preserve the most crucial information. This not only empowers machine learning models to operate more efficiently but also aids in data visualization and interpretability. Let's delve into two prominent dimensionality reduction techniques: Principal Component Analysis (PCA) and Linear Discriminant Analysis (LDA).

Principal Component Analysis (PCA):

Imagine a vast, high-dimensional landscape of data points. PCA acts as a skilled explorer, mapping this landscape and uncovering its underlying structure. It identifies the directions of greatest variance, essentially the most informative directions in the data. By projecting the data onto these principal components, PCA achieves dimensionality reduction while retaining the most significant information. This makes PCA a valuable tool for various tasks, including:

- Feature Extraction: PCA can identify a smaller set of features (principal components) that capture the essence of the data, allowing for more efficient model training and reduced computational cost.
- Data Visualization: By reducing dimensionality, PCA allows for easier visualization of complex datasets in lower-dimensional spaces, aiding in understanding the relationships between features.
- Noise Reduction: PCA can help mitigate the impact of noise in high-dimensional data by focusing on the directions of maximum variance, where the signal is strongest.

Linear Discriminant Analysis (LDA):

While PCA excels at general-purpose dimensionality reduction, LDA takes a more targeted approach specifically designed for classification tasks. Imagine you have data representing different classes, like emails categorized as spam or not spam. LDA aims to maximize the separation between these classes in the lower-dimensional space. It projects the data onto a subspace that best distinguishes between the classes, making it ideal for:

- Classification: By creating a well-separated representation of different classes, LDA empowers machine learning models to achieve better classification accuracy.
- Dimensionality Reduction for Classification: When dealing with high-dimensional classification problems, LDA offers a way to reduce dimensionality while preserving the information critical for class separation.

Choosing the Right Tool:

The best dimensionality reduction technique depends on your specific needs:

- General Dimensionality Reduction: If your goal is to reduce dimensionality for various purposes like visualization or feature extraction, PCA is a versatile choice.
- Dimensionality Reduction for Classification: When classification is the primary task, LDA is specifically designed to maximize class separation in the lower-dimensional space.

Beyond PCA and LDA:

While PCA and LDA are popular techniques, other dimensionality reduction methods exist, like t-distributed Stochastic Neighbour Embedding (t-SNE) for better preserving local data structure. The choice of technique depends on the specific characteristics of your data and the goals of your analysis.

In conclusion, dimensionality reduction techniques like PCA and LDA are powerful tools for navigating the complexities of high-dimensional data. By understanding their strengths and when to use them, you can empower your machine learning models and gain deeper insights from yourdata.

## CHAPTER SEVEN

FEATURE ENGINEERING FOR SPECIFIC TASKS

Feature engineering is a transformative process in machine learning, but it's not a universal recipe. The techniques you use can significantly impact your model's performance, and the best approach often hinges on the specific task at hand. For classification problems, you might focus on encoding categorical features and creating interaction features that capture relationships between existing ones. In regression tasks, feature scaling and selecting the most relevant features become crucial. Natural Language Processing demands cleaning text data and extracting features that capture the essence and context of the words. By tailoring your feature engineering to the specific task, you empower your machine learning models to extract the most valuable information from your data, leading to more accurate and insightful results.

Feature engineering isn't a one-size-fits-all approach in machine learning. The way you engineer features can significantly impact the performance of your model, and the optimal techniques often depend on the specific task at hand. Here's a breakdown of how feature engineering can be tailored to different tasks:

Classification Tasks:

Categorical Feature Encoding: When dealing with categorical features like customer type (bronze, silver, gold), encoding techniques like one-hot encoding or label encoding become crucial to transform these categories into numerical representations usable by machine learning models.

Feature Discretization: Continuous features like income or age can be discretized into bins (e.g., income brackets) to improve model performance, especially for algorithms that struggle with continuous data.

Interaction Feature Creation: Identifying and creating new features that capture the interaction between existing features can be particularly important in classification tasks. For example, in predicting loan defaults, the interaction between income level and credit score might be a stronger predictor than each feature alone.

Regression Tasks:

Feature Scaling: Normalizing features (like income or house size) to a common scale ensures all features contribute equally to the model and avoids issues with algorithms sensitive to feature magnitudes.

Feature Selection Techniques: Choosing the most relevant features that best predict the target variable (e.g., house price) is crucial. Techniques like filter methods or wrapper methods can help identify these informative features and streamline the model training process.

Deriving New Features: Domain knowledge can be valuable in creating new features specifically tailored to the regression task. For example, in predicting house prices, features like distance to amenities or school quality might be derived from existing data.

Natural Language Processing (NLP) Tasks:

Text Preprocessing: Cleaning text data by removing stop words (common words like "the" or "and") and stemming/lemmatization (reducing words to their root form) is essential for NLP tasks.

Feature Extraction Techniques: Techniques like Bag-of-Words or TF-IDF can be used to convert text data into numerical representations suitable for machine learning models. These techniques capture the frequency and importance of words within the text.

N-Grams: Capturing sequences of words (bigrams, trigrams) can be helpful in NLP tasks like sentiment analysis, where understanding the context of words is important.

By understanding these task-specific considerations in feature engineering, you can create a more informative and effective feature set, ultimately leading to better performance and more accurate predictions from your machine learning models. Remember, feature engineering is an art as much as a science, and experimentation with different techniques is often key to finding the optimal approach for your specific data and task.

FEATURES ENGINEERING FOR CLASSIFICATION PROBLEMS

Crafting effective features is paramount for successful classification models in machine learning. Categorical features, like customer types (bronze, silver, gold), need special attention. Feature engineering techniques such as one-hot encoding or label encoding bridge the gap, transforming these categories into numerical data usable by the model. Continuous features like income or age can also benefit from feature engineering. Discretization, which groups continuous values into bins (e.g., income brackets), can improve model performance, especially for algorithms that struggle with raw, continuous data. But the magic truly happens when you explore interactions. Feature engineering allows you to create new features that capture the interplay between existing ones. In predicting loan defaults, for instance, the interaction between income level and credit score might be a stronger predictor than each feature alone. By strategically applying these feature engineering techniques, you can transform raw data into a powerful feature set that empowers your classification models to make accurate and insightful predictions.

In machine learning, classification tasks involve predicting a discrete category for new data points. Feature engineering plays a crucial role in this process by transforming raw data into features that are most informative for the classification model. Here's a breakdown of key feature engineering techniques for classification problems:

1. Handling Categorical Features:

Real-world data often includes categorical features like customer type (bronze, silver, gold) or product category (electronics, clothing). These features can't be directly processed by machine learning models that work with numerical data. Feature engineering techniques bridge this gap:

One-Hot Encoding: This method creates a new binary feature for each category. For example, "customer_type_bronze," "customer_type_silver," and "customer_type_gold" would be created for the customer type feature.

Label Encoding: This assigns a numerical value to each category. While simpler, it assumes an order between categories (e.g., bronze = 1, silver = 2), which might not always be true.

2. Taming Continuous Features:

While continuous features like income or age can be valuable, they might not be optimal in their raw form. Feature engineering helps us refine them:

Discretization: This groups continuous values into intervals (bins). For example, income could be divided into brackets like "< $30,000," "$30,000 - $50,000," etc. Discretization can improve model performance, especially for algorithms that struggle with continuous data.

3. The Power of Interactions:

Not all features act independently. Feature engineering allows you to create new features that capture the interaction between existing ones. Imagine predicting loan defaults. The interaction between income level and credit score might be a stronger predictor than each feature alone. Techniques like:

- Multiplication: Multiplying existing features creates a new feature representing their interaction.
- Domain Knowledge: Based on your understanding of the problem, you can create new features that capture specific interactions.

Benefits of Feature Engineering for Classification:

- Improved Model Performance: By providing more informative features, feature engineering can significantly improve the accuracy and generalizability of your classification models.
- Reduced Overfitting: Well-engineered features can help the model learn the underlying patterns in the data rather than just memorizing specifics, leading to better performance on unseen data.
- Enhanced Model Interpretability: When features are carefully crafted and have clear meaning, it's easier to understand how the model makes its predictions.

Remember, feature engineering is an iterative process. Experiment with different techniques and evaluate their impact on your model's performance.

TECHNIQUES FOR TEXT CLASSIFICATION

There are several techniques for text classification, ranging from rule-based systems to advanced machine learning algorithms. Rule-based systems rely on manually crafted rules to identify specific keywords or patterns that indicate a certain category. Machine learning, on the other hand, can automatically learn these patterns from labeled training data. Popular machine learning techniques for text classification include Naive Bayes, Support Vector Machines, and Deep Learning models like Convolutional Neural Networks and Recurrent Neural Networks. The choice of technique depends on factors like the amount of labeled data available and the specific classification task.

Text classification is the process of assigning predefined categories or labels to text data. It's a fundamental task in Natural Language Processing (NLP) with applications spanning sentiment analysis, spam filtering, topic modeling, and more. Techniques for text classification can be broadly categorized into:

Rule-based systems: These rely on human-defined rules and patterns to categorize text. While effective for specific domains, they can be rigid and require significant manual effort.

Machine learning: This approach leverages algorithms to automatically learn patterns from labeled data. Popular techniques include Naive Bayes, Support Vector Machines (SVM), and Decision Trees. These methods excel at handling large datasets and adapting to new patterns.

Deep learning: This cutting-edge approach employs neural networks to extract complex features from text. Models like Convolutional Neural Networks (CNN) and Recurrent Neural Networks (RNN) have shown remarkable performance in text classification tasks, especially for handling long-range dependencies and semantic nuances.

The choice of technique depends on factors such as the size and quality of the dataset, the complexity of the classification task, and the desired level of accuracy. Hybrid approaches combining multiple techniques often yield improved results.

FEATURE ENGINEERING FOR IMAGE RECOGNITION

Feature engineering is particularly crucial in image recognition. Unlike structured data, images are complex arrays of pixels that require careful transformation into meaningful features for models to understand. This process involves extracting relevant information such as edges, corners, textures, and color histograms. By crafting these representative features, data scientists enable algorithms to discriminate between different image categories, detect objects within scenes, or recognize faces with remarkable accuracy. In the realm of image recognition, feature engineering involves transforming raw pixel data into informative representations that a machine learning model can effectively process. [1] This crucial step is akin to teaching a computer to "see" and understand visual patterns. By extracting relevant features such as edges, corners, textures, and color distributions, data scientists create a foundation for models to learn and classify images accurately.For instance, in facial recognition, features like eye distance, nose shape, and jawline contours are essential for distinguishing individuals. Similarly, identifying objects in images often relies on features like shape, size, and spatial relationships between elements.

The Challenge of Raw Image Data

Images are essentially matrices of pixel values, a format that is challenging for machines to interpret directly. To extract meaningful information, feature engineering is indispensable. This process transforms raw pixel data into numerical representations that capture essential visual characteristics.

Extracting Meaningful Features

Low-Level Features: These are basic image properties like edges, corners, and textures. They are often obtained using techniques like edge detection, corner detection, and filter banks.

Mid-Level Features: Building upon low-level features, mid-level features represent more complex patterns like shapes, objects, and parts. Techniques like SIFT (Scale-Invariant Feature Transform) and HOG (Histogram of Oriented Gradients) are commonly used.

High-Level Features: These features capture semantic information and are often domain-specific. For instance, in facial recognition, features like eye distance, nose shape, and mouth curvature would be considered high-level.

The Role of Feature Engineering in Image Recognition Tasks

- **Object Detection:** By extracting features that represent objects of interest, models can accurately locate and classify objects within images.
- **Image Classification:** Feature engineering helps models discriminate between different image categories based on distinctive visual characteristics.
- **Image Segmentation:** By identifying and delineating objects or regions within an image, feature engineering aids in image segmentation tasks.
- **Image Retrieval:** Relevant features enable efficient searching and retrieval of similar images from large databases.

The Evolution of Feature Engineering

While traditional methods have been effective, deep learning has revolutionized feature engineering. Convolutional Neural Networks (CNNs) automatically learn hierarchical features from raw image data, reducing the manual effort required. However, domain-specific knowledge and handcrafted features can still complement deep learning models, enhancing performance in specific tasks.

FEATURE ENGINEERING FOR TIME SERIES FORECASTING

Feature engineering is a cornerstone of effective time series forecasting. By transforming raw data into informative features, practitioners can extract valuable insights and improve model performance. This process involves creating new variables that capture underlying patterns, trends, and relationships within the data. Through careful consideration of factors such as seasonality, trend, and external influences, feature engineering empowers models to make more accurate predictions.

Feature engineering is a critical step in building accurate time series forecasting models. It involves transforming raw time series data into informative features that capture underlying patterns and trends. This process is essential for extracting meaningful information from the data and providing valuable inputs to machine learning algorithms.

By creating relevant features, you can improve model performance significantly. For example, incorporating lagged values of the target variable can capture historical patterns, while calculating moving averages can smooth out noise and reveal underlying trends. Additionally, time-based features such as day of the week, month, or holiday indicators can help capture seasonal variations.

Effective feature engineering requires a deep understanding of the data, the underlying processes, and the forecasting problem at hand. It's often an iterative process involving experimentation and evaluation to determine the most impactful features.

Common feature engineering techniques include:

Lagged variables: Incorporating past values of the target variable as features can capture trends and seasonality. For instance, using previous day's sales to predict today's sales can reveal sales patterns.

Moving averages: Smoothing out noise in the data by calculating averages over a specific window size. This helps to identify underlying trends more clearly.

Exponential smoothing: Assigns exponentially decreasing weights to past observations, giving more weight to recent data. This method is effective for capturing trends and seasonality.

Differencing: Reducing trends or seasonality by subtracting the value from a previous time step. This can help stabilize the time series and make it stationary.

Time-based features: Creating features based on time components like hour, day, week, month, or year can capture cyclical patterns. For example, hourly data can reveal daily patterns.

External variables: Incorporating relevant external factors like weather, economic indicators, or holidays can improve forecast accuracy by accounting for external influences on the target variable.

The predictive power of your time series models and gain deeper insights into the underlying patterns of your data.

Lagged Variables:

One of the most fundamental feature engineering techniques for time series forecasting is creating lagged variables. These are essentially past values of the target variable used as predictors for future values.

Use Of lagged variables

- Capturing temporal dependencies: Lagged variables help capture the underlying patterns and relationships between past and future values.
- Identifying trends and seasonality: By examining the correlations between lagged variables and the target variable, you can uncover trends, seasonal patterns, and cyclical

components.

- Improving model performance: Incorporating lagged variables often significantly enhances the predictive power of time series models.

Lag order selection: Determining the optimal number of lags to include is crucial. Too few lags might miss important patterns, while too many can introduce noise and overfitting.

Stationarity: Lagged variables can introduce autocorrelation, which can violate the stationarity assumption of many time series models. Differencing or other transformations might be necessary.

Feature importance: Not all lagged variables will contribute equally to the model. Feature selection techniques can help identify the most relevant lags.

Example: In forecasting product sales, using previous day, week, and month sales as lagged variables can help capture daily, weekly, and monthly sales patterns. These features can then be used to train a model to predict future sales.

- Differenced lags: Creating lagged differences can help capture changes in the data over time.
- Lagged transformations: Applying transformations like logarithms or square roots to lagged variables can sometimes improve model performance.

By effectively utilizing lagged variables, you can build more robust and accurate time series forecasting models.

## CHAPTER EIGHT

ADVANCED FEATURE ENGINEERING TECHNIQUES

While basic feature engineering techniques, such as scaling, encoding, and handling missing values, form the foundation, advanced techniques are often required to unlock the full potential of complex datasets. These methods involve sophisticated transformations, domain expertise, and a deep understanding of the problem at hand. Advanced feature engineering goes beyond simple data manipulation and aims to create features that capture intricate patterns, non-linear relationships, and hidden information within the data. By employing these techniques, practitioners can significantly enhance model performance and gain deeper insights into the underlying phenomena.

FEATURE ENGINEERING WITH NATURAL LANGUAGE PROCESSING (NLP)

Feature engineering in Natural Language Processing (NLP) is the art and science of transforming raw text data into numerical representations that can be effectively processed by machine learning algorithms. Unlike structured data, text is inherently unstructured and requires careful manipulation to extract meaningful features. This process involves a combination of linguistic knowledge, domain expertise, and data-driven techniques. By crafting informative features, practitioners can enhance the performance of NLP models for tasks such as text classification, sentiment analysis, and information retrieval.

Feature engineering in NLP is the process of converting raw text data into numerical representations suitable for machine learning algorithms. Unlike structured data, text is inherently unstructured, making it challenging to directly feed into models. This transformation is crucial for tasks like sentiment analysis, text classification, and information retrieval.

Text Preprocessing

The initial step involves cleaning and preparing the text data. This includes tasks such as:

- Tokenization: Breaking down text into individual words or subwords.
- Stop word removal: Eliminating common words that add little semantic value (e.g., "the," "and," "of").
- Stemming and Lemmatization: Reducing words to their root form to improve feature representation.
- Lowercasing: Converting text to lowercase for consistency.
- Handling special characters and punctuation: Removing or replacing special characters as needed.

Text Representation

Once the text is preprocessed, it needs to be converted into numerical vectors. Common techniques include:

- Bag of Words (BoW): Representing documents as a count of word occurrences.
- Term Frequency-Inverse Document Frequency (TF-IDF): Weighing words based on their frequency within and across documents.
- N-grams: Considering sequences of words as features.
- Word Embeddings: Representing words as dense vectors capturing semantic and syntactic relationships (e.g., Word2Vec,

GloVe).

Advanced Techniques

For more complex NLP tasks, advanced feature engineering techniques are often employed:

- Part-of-Speech (POS) tagging: Identifying the grammatical role of words.
- Named Entity Recognition (NER): Extracting entities like persons, organizations, and locations.
- Dependency Parsing: Analyzing grammatical relationships between words.
- Sentiment Analysis Features: Deriving sentiment-related features (e.g., polarity, subjectivity).

By carefully selecting and combining these techniques, practitioners can create informative features that enhance the performance of NLP models

FEATURE ENGINEERING FOR RECOMMENDER SYSTEMS

Feature engineering is a critical component of building effective recommender systems. By carefully crafting informative features from user, item, and interaction data, practitioners can enhance the ability of models to accurately predict user preferences and generate relevant recommendations. This process involves transforming raw data into meaningful representations that capture user behavior, item attributes, and contextual information, ultimately driving improved recommendation quality and user satisfaction.

User and Item Features

A cornerstone of feature engineering for recommender systems involves creating features that represent users and items. These features serve as the foundation for understanding user preferences and item attributes.

User Features

Demographic Information:

Age, gender, location, occupation, and other relevant demographic data can help identify user segments with similar preferences. For example, a music recommender system might suggest different genres based on a user's age.

Importance: These features provide a basic understanding of the user and can be used for initial segmentation.

Behavioral Data:

Features derived from user interactions, such as purchase history, browsing behavior, search queries, and ratings, provide insights into user interests and preferences. For instance, a movie recommender system can suggest similar movies based on a user's previous ratings.

This data is crucial for understanding user preferences and is often the backbone of collaborative filtering-based recommenders.

Temporal Features:

Information about user activity patterns over time, including time of day, day of week, and seasonality, can capture user habits and preferences. For example, a food delivery app might suggest different cuisines based on the time of day.

Importance: Understanding temporal patterns can help in recommending items relevant to specific time periods.

Social Features:

Incorporating social connections, friend recommendations, and group memberships can leverage social influence for recommendations. For example, a social media platform might suggest friends' posts or products based on their interactions.

Importance: Social features can significantly enhance recommendation accuracy, especially in platforms with a strong social component.

Item Features

Content-Based Features:

Textual descriptions, categories, genres, keywords, and other content-related attributes can help identify similar items. For example, a book recommender system might suggest books with similar genres or authors.

Content-based features are essential for content-based recommendation systems and can be used to enrich collaborative filtering approaches.

Visual Features:

Image and video content can be analyzed to extract visual features like color, texture, and object recognition. For example, a fashion recommender system might suggest similar items based on visual similarity.

Visual features are crucial for image-based recommendation systems and can enhance the overall recommendation quality.

Collaborative Filtering Features:

Implicit or explicit ratings from other users can be used to generate item-based collaborative filtering features. For example, a movie recommender system can suggest movies that similar users have liked.

Collaborative filtering features are fundamental for collaborative filtering-based recommenders and can be combined with other feature types.

Metadata Features:

Additional information about items, such as price, release date, and brand, can provide valuable context. For example, a product recommender system might suggest items within a specific price range.

Metadata features can help refine recommendations based on user preferences and item attributes.

By effectively combining user and item features, recommender systems can generate personalized recommendations that align with user preferences and item characteristics.

LEVERAGING FEATURE STORES FOR SCALABLE FEATURE ENGINEERING

Feature engineering is the backbone of successful machine learning models, but it can be a time-consuming and error-prone process. Traditionally, data scientists and engineers spend significant effort creating, managing, and serving features, often leading to inefficiencies and inconsistencies. To address these challenges, feature stores have emerged as a critical component of modern ML pipelines. By centralizing feature management, versioning, and serving, feature stores empower teams to accelerate model development, improve collaboration, and ensure feature quality, ultimately driving better business outcomes.

The Challenge of Traditional Feature Engineering

Traditional feature engineering is a time-consuming and error-prone process. Data scientists and engineers often spend significant effort creating, managing, and serving features, leading to inefficiencies and inconsistencies. This manual approach can hinder the pace of model development and deployment.

## CHAPTER NINE

THE FEATURE ENGINEERING WORKFLOW

The feature engineering workflow encompasses a systematic process of transforming raw data into meaningful features that can be effectively utilized by machine learning models. It typically involves several key stages: data ingestion and exploration, feature creation and selection, feature transformation, and feature evaluation. During data ingestion, raw data is collected from various sources and undergoes initial cleaning and preprocessing.

Feature creation involves deriving new features from existing data or domain knowledge, while feature selection identifies the most relevant features for the model. Feature transformation applies techniques like scaling, normalization, and encoding to prepare features for model training. Finally, feature evaluation assesses the impact of engineered features on model performance to refine the process iteratively. Data scientists meticulously examine the dataset to uncover patterns, relationships, and potential features. Subsequently, they create new features or extract relevant information from existing data. Feature transformation techniques are applied to enhance feature representation and compatibility with machine learning algorithms. Through rigorous evaluation, the most impactful features are selected to build robust models. This workflow demands domain expertise, creativity, and experimentation to extract maximum value from the data.

ITERATIVE FEATUIRE ENGINEERING PROCESS

Feature engineering, the art of transforming raw data into meaningful features, is a critical yet often overlooked component of successful machine learning models. Unlike a linear process, feature engineering is fundamentally iterative, requiring continuous experimentation, refinement, and evaluation. By systematically cycling through stages of feature creation, transformation, selection, and evaluation, data scientists can unlock the full potential of their data and build high-performing models.

Feature Creation: This involves generating new features from existing data, often through domain knowledge, statistical techniques, or exploratory data analysis. Examples include creating interaction terms, deriving temporal features, or aggregating data into meaningful summaries.

Feature Transformation: This step focuses on modifying the distribution or scale of existing features to improve model performance. Common techniques include normalization, standardization, binning, and log transformations.

Feature Selection: Identifying the most relevant features is crucial for model efficiency and interpretability. Methods like correlation analysis, feature importance, and dimensionality reduction techniques help select the optimal subset of features.

Evaluation: The impact of feature engineering choices is assessed through rigorous model evaluation using appropriate metrics. Techniques like cross-validation, holdout validation, and A/B testing help measure feature effectiveness.

Iteration: The process is cyclical, with insights from evaluation feeding back into feature creation, transformation, and selection. This iterative approach allows for continuous improvement and optimization of the feature set.

EVALUATING FEATURE ENGINEERING EFFECTIVENESS

valuating the effectiveness of feature engineering is crucial for optimizing model performance. It involves a systematic assessment of the impact of engineered features on the model's ability to make accurate predictions. Several key metrics and techniques can be employed to evaluate feature engineering effectiveness:

Model Performance Metrics:

Traditional metrics: Accuracy, precision, recall, F1-score, ROC curve, AUC, etc., are used to assess the overall performance of the model.

Regression metrics: Mean Squared Error (MSE), Root Mean Squared Error (RMSE), Mean Absolute Error (MAE), R-squared, etc., are relevant for regression problems.

Feature Importance:

Model-based techniques: Random Forest, Gradient Boosting, and other tree-based models provide feature importance scores.

Correlation analysis: Measuring the correlation between features and the target variable can identify potentially informative features.

Cross-Validation:

Assessing model performance on different subsets of data helps to prevent overfitting and provides a more reliable estimate of generalization error.

A/B Testing:

Comparing models with different feature sets on real-world data can provide insights into the impact of feature engineering on business outcomes.

Feature Visualization:

Visualizing feature distributions, correlations, and relationships with the target variable can help identify potential issues and opportunities for improvement.

By combining these evaluation methods, data scientists can gain valuable insights into the effectiveness of their feature engineering efforts and make data-driven decisions to optimize model performance.

BEST PRATICES FOR FEATURE ENGINEERING

Effective feature engineering is crucial for building high-performing machine learning models. Here are some key best practices:

Understand the Problem and Data

- Domain Knowledge: A deep understanding of the problem domain is essential for creating relevant features.
- Exploratory Data Analysis (EDA): Thoroughly analyze the data to identify patterns, trends, and potential features.
- Data Quality: Ensure data is clean, consistent, and free from errors or missing values.

Feature Creation and Selection

- Feature Relevance: Create features that are directly related to the target variable.
- Feature Interaction: Consider how features interact with each other to create new informative features.
- Feature Scaling: Standardize or normalize features to improve model performance.
- Dimensionality Reduction: Apply techniques like PCA or t-SNE to reduce the number of features while preserving information.
- Feature Selection: Employ methods like correlation analysis, feature importance, or regularization to select the most relevant features.

Iterative Process

- Experimentation: Test different feature combinations and transformations to find the optimal set.
- Evaluation: Continuously evaluate the impact of features on model performance using appropriate metrics.
- Refinement: Iterate on feature engineering based on evaluation results.

Additional Considerations

- Feature Documentation: Maintain clear documentation of feature creation and transformation processes.
- Feature Store: Consider using a feature store for efficient management and reuse of features.
- Automation: Automate feature engineering pipelines for scalability and reproducibility.
- Explainability: Create features that are interpretable to enhance model understanding.

By following these best practices, you can significantly improve the performance and reliability of your machine learning models.

Encoding Techniques

Categorical data, which represents categories or labels rather than numerical values, requires encoding before being fed into most machine learning algorithms. Here are common encoding techniques:

One-Hot Encoding:

- Converts each category into a binary feature.
- Suitable for nominal categorical variables with no inherent order.
- Can lead to high dimensionality if there are many categories.
- Example: Color with categories Red, Green, Blue becomes three binary features: Red (0,1,0), Green (0,0,1), Blue (1,0,0).

Label Encoding:

- Assigns a unique integer to each category.
- Suitable for ordinal categorical variables with a clear order.
- Should be used cautiously as it can introduce an artificial order into nominal data.
- Example: Size with categories Small, Medium, Large becomes 0, 1, 2.

Target Encoding:

- Replaces each category with the mean (or other statistic) of the target variable for that category.
- Captures the relationship between the categorical feature and the target variable.
- Can lead to overfitting if not handled carefully.
- Example: If predicting house prices, replace "City" with the average house price in that city.

Handling High Cardinality Categorical Variables

High cardinality categorical features (with many unique values) can pose challenges. Here are some techniques:

Frequency Encoding: Replace categories with their frequency in the dataset.

Grouping: Combine infrequent categories into a single category (e.g., "Other").

Hashing: Map categories to a fixed number of buckets using a hash function.

Embedding: Learn dense representations of categorical variables using techniques like embedding layers in neural networks.

Feature Engineering for Categorical Data

Creating new features based on categorical data can improve model performance. Some techniques include:

- Interaction features: Combine categorical features with other features (numeric or categorical) to capture interactions.
- Grouping and binning: Group categorical values based on similarity or create bins for numerical features.
- Time-based features: Extract time-related information from categorical features (e.g., day of week, month).
- Feature crossing: Combine multiple categorical features to create new features.

Choosing the right encoding technique and feature engineering approach depends on the specific dataset, problem, and model used. Experimentation and evaluation are crucial to find the best approach.

## CHAPTER TEN

FEATURE ENGINEERING IN THE REAL WORLD

Feature engineering is the unsung hero of successful machine learning models. While algorithms and computing power garner significant attention, the quality and relevance of features extracted from raw data often determine a model's predictive power. In the real world, data is messy, incomplete, and often irrelevant. Feature engineering involves transforming this raw data into informative and meaningful features that can be effectively utilized by machine learning algorithms. This critical process requires a blend of domain expertise, statistical knowledge, and creativity to extract valuable insights and build robust models.

CASE STUDIES IN FEATURE ENGINEERING FOR DIFFERENT APPLICATION

Case studies illuminate the transformative power of feature engineering across diverse domains. From financial modeling to healthcare diagnostics, carefully crafted features have been instrumental in driving model performance. For instance, in fraud detection, engineered features capturing transaction patterns and user behavior have significantly improved model accuracy. Similarly, in the realm of precision medicine, extracting meaningful features from patient data has enabled the development of personalized treatment plans. These real-world examples underscore the critical role of feature engineering in unlocking the full potential of machine learning algorithms.

Financial Services

In the realm of financial services, feature engineering has proven to be a game-changer. For instance, in fraud detection, creating features that capture unusual transaction patterns, such as large purchases in unfamiliar locations or sudden changes in spending habits, has significantly improved model accuracy. Additionally, in credit risk assessment, engineered features derived from customer demographics, financial history, and behavioral data have enabled more precise risk predictions.

The financial services industry is heavily reliant on data-driven decision-making. Feature engineering plays a pivotal role in transforming raw financial data into actionable insights.

Fraud Detection

Fraudulent activities pose a significant threat to financial institutions. By carefully crafting features that highlight unusual transaction patterns, models can be trained to identify suspicious behavior. For instance:

- **Transaction anomalies:** Features such as large, unexpected purchases, transactions from unusual locations, or multiple transactions within a short timeframe can indicate fraudulent activity.
- **Velocity and frequency:** Analyzing the speed and frequency of transactions can help identify patterns associated with fraudsters.
- **Behavioral patterns:** Features capturing changes in customer behavior, such as sudden increases in spending or new types of transactions, can be indicative of fraudulent account takeover.

By incorporating these features into machine learning models, financial institutions can significantly improve their ability to detect and prevent fraud.

Credit Risk Assessment

Accurate credit risk assessment is essential for lending institutions. Feature engineering empowers models to make more informed decisions by extracting relevant information from customer data:

- **Demographic features:** Factors such as age, occupation, income, and location can influence creditworthiness.
- **Financial history:** Features related to past credit behavior, including payment history, credit utilization, and loan repayment performance, provide valuable insights.
- **Behavioral features:** Analyzing customer behavior, such as spending patterns, savings habits, and bill payment history, can help assess credit risk.
- **Macroeconomic indicators:** Incorporating economic factors like interest rates, unemployment rates, and GDP can account for broader economic trends affecting credit risk.

By combining these features, models can more accurately predict the likelihood of default and inform lending decisions.

Healthcare

The healthcare industry has witnessed the transformative power of feature engineering. For instance, in medical image analysis, extracting relevant features from X-rays, MRIs, and CT scans has facilitated accurate diagnosis of diseases like cancer and pneumonia. Moreover, in patient data analysis, creating features that capture patient history, lab results, and vital signs has supported the development of predictive models for disease outbreaks and patient outcomes.

The healthcare industry is undergoing a digital transformation, with data playing a crucial role in improving patient outcomes and driving efficiency. Feature engineering is at the heart of this transformation, enabling the extraction of valuable insights from complex healthcare data.

Medical Image Analysis

Medical imaging techniques generate vast amounts of data, which can be challenging to interpret manually. Feature engineering transforms raw image data into meaningful representations that facilitate accurate diagnosis and treatment planning. For example:

- **Texture analysis:** By quantifying image textures, features can be extracted to identify abnormalities in organs and tissues.
- **Shape analysis:** Analyzing the shape of structures within images can help detect tumors, lesions, or other irregularities.
- **Intensity-based features:** Extracting information about pixel intensities can aid in differentiating between healthy and diseased tissues.

By combining these features, machine learning models can be trained to accurately classify medical images, detect diseases, and assist in treatment planning.

Patient Data Analysis

Electronic health records (EHRs) contain a wealth of patient information, including demographics, medical history, lab results, and vital signs. Feature engineering helps uncover hidden patterns and trends within this data:

- **Patient history:** Creating features based on past diagnoses, medications, and procedures can identify risk factors for certain diseases.
- **Lab results:** Extracting relevant information from lab tests can help monitor disease progression and treatment effectiveness.
- **Vital signs:** Analyzing trends in blood pressure, heart rate, and other vital signs can detect early signs of deterioration.

By transforming patient data into informative features, predictive models can be developed to anticipate disease outbreaks, optimize treatment plans, and improve patient outcomes.

Feature engineering in healthcare has the potential to revolutionize patient care by enabling early disease detection, personalized treatment, and improved healthcare delivery.

Marketing and E-commerce

Feature engineering has been a catalyst for success in marketing and e-commerce. In customer segmentation, features derived from purchase history, browsing behavior, and demographic information have helped identify distinct customer groups for targeted marketing campaigns. Furthermore, in recommendation systems, creating features that capture user preferences, item attributes, and contextual information has enhanced the accuracy of product recommendations.

Feature engineering has become a cornerstone of successful marketing and e-commerce strategies. By transforming raw customer data into meaningful features, businesses can gain valuable insights and optimize their operations.

Customer Segmentation

Understanding customer segments is crucial for targeted marketing campaigns. Feature engineering plays a vital role in creating these segments by identifying distinct customer groups based on various attributes:

- **Demographic features:** Age, gender, location, income, and education level can be used to create basic customer segments.
- **Purchase history:** Analyzing past purchases, purchase frequency, and average order value can reveal spending patterns and preferences.
- **Browsing behavior:** Tracking website interactions, product views, and cart abandonment can provide insights into customer interests and needs.
- **Lifetime value (LTV):** Calculating customer LTV based on purchase history and engagement metrics helps identify high-value customers.

By combining these features, businesses can create detailed customer profiles and tailor marketing messages accordingly.

Recommendation Systems

Effective recommendation systems rely on accurate predictions of user preferences. Feature engineering helps capture the complexities of user-item interactions:

- User features: Information about users, such as demographics, purchase history, and browsing behavior, can be used to understand their preferences.
- Item features: Product attributes like category, brand, price, and reviews can be used to describe products effectively.
- Contextual features: Factors such as time, location, and weather can influence user behavior and product relevance.
- Interaction features: Information about past user-item interactions, such as ratings, purchases, and clicks, can be used to measure user interest.

By combining these features, recommendation algorithms can generate personalized product suggestions, increasing customer satisfaction and sales. Feature engineering in marketing and e-commerce empowers businesses to make data-driven decisions, improve customer experiences, and drive revenue growth.

The impact of feature engineering extends beyond these sectors. In the automotive industry, features derived from sensor data have enabled advanced driver assistance systems and autonomous vehicles. In agriculture, extracting features from satellite imagery and weather data has improved crop yield prediction and disease detection.

he transformative power of feature engineering extends far beyond the sectors we've discussed thus far. Its applications are vast and varied, driving innovation across multiple industries.

Automotive Industry

The automotive industry is undergoing a radical transformation with the advent of autonomous vehicles and advanced driver assistance systems (ADAS). Feature engineering plays a crucial role in extracting meaningful information from sensor data:

- **Sensor fusion:** Combining data from various sensors, such as cameras, lidar, radar, and GPS, requires careful feature engineering to create a unified and accurate representation of the environment.

- **Object detection and tracking:** Extracting features from sensor data enables the identification and tracking of vehicles, pedestrians, and other road users.
- **Predictive modeling:** By creating features that capture vehicle dynamics, driver behavior, and road conditions, predictive models can be developed to anticipate potential hazards and improve safety.

Feature engineering is essential for developing robust and reliable autonomous vehicles.

Agriculture

Precision agriculture relies heavily on data-driven insights to optimize crop yields and resource utilization. Feature engineering plays a vital role in extracting valuable information from agricultural data:

- **Satellite imagery:** Analyzing satellite images to extract features related to crop health, soil conditions, and vegetation indices can help monitor crop growth and identify potential issues.
- **Weather data:** Incorporating weather information, such as temperature, rainfall, and humidity, into feature engineering models can help predict crop yields and optimize irrigation schedules.
- **Sensor data:** Using data from soil sensors, drones, and other devices, features can be extracted to monitor soil moisture, nutrient levels, and crop conditions.

By effectively utilizing feature engineering, farmers can make informed decisions to increase productivity and sustainability.

These examples demonstrate the broad applicability of feature engineering across diverse industries. As data continues to grow in volume and complexity, the importance of feature engineering will only increase, driving innovation and creating new opportunities.

These case studies highlight the versatility and importance of feature engineering in driving innovation and solving complex problems across various industries.

CHALLENGES AND CONSIDERATION FOR REAL-WORLD FEATURE ENGINEERING

Real-world feature engineering is a complex endeavor fraught with challenges. Data quality issues, such as missing values, outliers, and inconsistencies, often hinder the feature creation process. Additionally, understanding the underlying domain knowledge is crucial for selecting relevant features, but this expertise is not always readily available. Furthermore, the curse of dimensionality can arise as the number of features grows, leading to computational inefficiency and overfitting. Balancing the trade-off between feature complexity and model performance is another critical consideration. To address these challenges, a combination of domain expertise, statistical techniques, and iterative experimentation is essential.

Data Quality Issues

Real-world data is often far from perfect, presenting several challenges that can significantly impact the quality of derived features and, subsequently, the performance of machine learning models.

Missing Values

Incomplete data is a common issue, where certain values are absent for specific data points. This can occur due to various reasons, such as data entry errors, equipment failures, or privacy concerns. Missing values can distort statistical measures and lead to biased models if not handled appropriately.

Outliers

Outliers are data points that deviate significantly from the overall pattern. These can be genuine anomalies or errors in data collection. Outliers can have a disproportionate influence on statistical models and can mask underlying patterns.

Inconsistencies

Data inconsistency arises when the same information is represented differently across various data sources or within the same dataset. This can include variations in data formats, units, or coding schemes. Inconsistent data can lead to erroneous calculations and misleading insights.

Noise

Noise refers to random errors or fluctuations in the data that can obscure underlying patterns. It can originate from various sources, including measurement errors, environmental factors, or data transmission issues. Noise can reduce the reliability of features and hinder model performance.

Duplicates

Duplicate data refers to identical or near-identical data points that exist within a dataset. Duplicates can inflate sample sizes, leading to biased estimates and reduced model accuracy.

Addressing these data quality issues is a crucial initial step in the feature engineering process. Techniques such as imputation, outlier detection, data standardization, and data cleaning are essential to ensure data reliability and improve the quality of derived features.

Domain Expertise Requirement

A deep understanding of the problem domain is paramount for successful feature engineering. Domain knowledge provides invaluable insights into: Identifying features that are directly connected to the target variable. Without domain expertise, there's a risk of including irrelevant features that add noise and computational overhead without improving model performance. Understanding how different variables interact can lead to the creation of powerful composite features. Domain experts can often suggest potential combinations of features that might be predictive. Interpreting the meaning of features and their relationship to the problem is crucial for understanding model behavior and making informed decisions. Domain knowledge helps in translating model outputs into actionable insights. Collaboration between data scientists and domain experts is essential to bridge the gap between technical knowledge and real-world understanding.

Curse of Dimensionality and Overfitting

As the number of features in a dataset grows, the dimensionality of the data increases, leading to several challenges:With a large number of features, models become computationally expensive to train and make predictions. This can hinder model development and deployment. High-dimensional spaces can lead to models that are too complex and capture noise in the data rather than underlying patterns. This results in poor generalization performance.

To mitigate these issues, feature selection and dimensionality reduction techniques are employed: Identifies the most relevant features and discards irrelevant ones, improving model efficiency and reducing overfitting.Projects the data into a lower-dimensional space while preserving essential information, making it computationally feasible and reducing the risk of overfitting. By carefully selecting and transforming features, it's possible to overcome the curse of dimensionality and build more effective models.

## CHAPTER ELEVEN

THE FUTURE OF FEATURE ENGINEERING

The future of feature engineering promises a dynamic landscape where human ingenuity and artificial intelligence converge. As data volumes continue to explode and model complexity grows, the traditional, manual approach to feature engineering will likely evolve. We can anticipate advancements in automation, where algorithms will increasingly assist in feature generation and selection. However, human expertise will remain indispensable for guiding these processes and ensuring that features align with real-world understanding. Ultimately, the future of feature engineering will be characterized by a symbiotic relationship between humans and machines, working collaboratively to extract maximum value from data. As datasets grow exponentially in size and diversity, the manual crafting of features is becoming increasingly challenging and time-consuming. Consequently, there is a growing emphasis on automating feature engineering processes, leveraging advanced algorithms, and integrating domain knowledge seamlessly. The convergence of artificial intelligence and feature engineering holds the promise of creating more intelligent and efficient systems capable of extracting valuable insights from raw data with unprecedented accuracy. This has spurred the development of automated feature engineering tools and algorithms, promising to streamline the process and unlock new possibilities. Moreover, the integration of domain expertise with advanced computational methods will be crucial for creating features that not only improve model performance but also enhance interpretability and explainability.

EMERGING TRENDS IN FEATURE ENGINEERING

Emerging trends in feature engineering are reshaping the landscape of data-driven applications. Automated feature engineering, leveraging techniques like AutoML and neural architecture search, is gaining prominence, reducing manual effort and accelerating model development. Additionally, the integration of deep learning for feature extraction is unlocking new possibilities, especially in domains like image and natural language processing. A growing emphasis on feature interpretability and explainability is driving the development of techniques that shed light on the decision-making process of models. Furthermore, the incorporation of contextual information and domain-specific knowledge is becoming increasingly crucial for creating effective and robust features.

The field of feature engineering is rapidly evolving, driven by advancements in machine learning and the increasing complexity of data. Several key trends are shaping the future of feature engineering:

Automated Feature Engineering

Leveraging techniques like AutoML and neural architecture search, automated tools are being developed to streamline the feature engineering process, reducing manual effort and accelerating model development. Automated feature engineering is a rapidly evolving field that aims to automate the process of creating informative features from raw data. By leveraging techniques like AutoML and neural architecture search, these tools significantly reduce the manual effort required by data scientists.

AutoML: AutoML platforms encompass a broad range of automated machine learning capabilities, including feature engineering. They employ algorithms to explore different feature combinations, transformations, and selections, often guided by optimization techniques.

Neural Architecture Search: While primarily used for designing neural network architectures, this technique can also be adapted for feature engineering. By automatically searching for optimal feature representations, neural architecture search can discover complex and informative features.

The benefits of automated feature engineering include:

- **Increased efficiency:** Automating the feature engineering process saves time and resources.
- **Improved performance:** Automated tools can explore a vast feature space and potentially discover high-quality features that humans might overlook.
- **Reduced bias:** By removing human bias from the feature engineering process, automated tools can help create fairer and more equitable models.

While automated feature engineering is a promising approach, it's essential to combine it with human expertise to ensure that the generated features are interpretable and aligned with domain knowledge.

Deep Learning for Feature Extraction

Deep learning models, particularly convolutional neural networks (CNNs) and recurrent neural networks (RNNs), are being employed to extract high-level features directly from raw data, bypassing traditional hand-crafted feature engineering. Deep learning has revolutionized feature extraction by automating the process of learning meaningful representations directly from raw data.

Unlike traditional hand-crafted features, which require domain expertise and significant effort, deep learning models can learn complex patterns and hierarchies of features.

- **Convolutional Neural Networks (CNNs):** Primarily used for image and computer vision tasks, CNNs excel at extracting hierarchical features. The initial layers capture low-level features like edges and textures, while deeper layers learn more abstract representations like shapes and objects.

- **Recurrent Neural Networks (RNNs):** Designed for sequential data, RNNs can capture temporal dependencies and extract features that represent patterns over time. They are commonly used in natural language processing and time series analysis.

By eliminating the need for manual feature engineering, deep learning models often achieve superior performance on a wide range of tasks. However, it's important to note that deep learning models can be computationally expensive and require large amounts of data to train effectively. Additionally, interpreting the learned features can be challenging, limiting their explainability compared to hand-crafted features.

Feature Interpretability and Explainability: There's a growing emphasis on understanding how features contribute to model predictions. Techniques like SHAP (SHapley Additive exPlanations) are gaining popularity to enhance model transparency and trust.

Contextual Feature Engineering: Incorporating contextual information, such as time, location, or user behavior, into feature engineering is becoming increasingly important to capture complex relationships and improve model performance.

Domain-Specific Feature Engineering: Tailoring feature engineering techniques to specific domains, such as healthcare or finance, is leading to the development of domain-specific feature libraries and best practices.

These trends are collectively driving the next generation of feature engineering, enabling the creation of more powerful and interpretable machine learning models.

Feature Interpretability and Explainability

As machine learning models become increasingly complex, the need for understanding their decision-making processes has grown significantly. Feature interpretability and explainability focus on deciphering how specific features contribute to model predictions.

This involves understanding the relationship between individual features and the model's output. By examining feature weights or coefficients, one can gain insights into which features are most important in driving predictions. This goes beyond understanding individual features and aims to explain how a combination of features contributes to a specific prediction. It involves techniques that quantify the impact of each feature on the model's output for a particular instance.

SHAP (SHapley Additive exPlanations) is a prominent technique for feature explainability. It assigns a value to each feature contributing to a prediction, representing the feature's importance in that specific case. SHAP values can be visualized to understand how different features collaborate to influence the model's decision.

Contextual Feature Engineering

Contextual feature engineering involves incorporating additional information about the data points into the feature set. By considering factors like time, location, or user behavior, it's possible to capture complex relationships and patterns that static features might miss.

- **Temporal features:** Incorporating time-related information, such as time of day, day of week, or season, can significantly improve model performance in time-series data or any dataset with a temporal component. For example, predicting energy consumption based on time of day and day of the week can be more accurate than using historical consumption alone.
- **Geographic features:** Incorporating location data, such as latitude, longitude, or zip code, can be crucial for models that deal with spatial data. For instance, predicting housing prices can benefit from including features related to proximity to schools, parks, or public transportation.
- **User behavior features:** Understanding user behavior can be invaluable for recommendation systems, fraud detection, and customer segmentation. Features like browsing history,

purchase history, or clickstream data can help capture user preferences and patterns.

Contextual feature engineering often requires domain expertise to identify relevant contextual factors and create effective features. It's essential to consider how these features interact with other variables and how they influence the target variable. By incorporating contextual information, models can become more accurate, interpretable, and adaptable to changing conditions.

THE ROLE OF AUTOMATION IN FEATURE ENGINEERING

The advent of automation has ushered in a new era for feature engineering, transforming it from a time-consuming, manual task into a more efficient and scalable process. As datasets grow exponentially in size and complexity, the need for automated tools to handle the deluge of data has become increasingly apparent. By automating routine tasks like data cleaning, feature creation, and selection, data scientists can devote more time to higher-level analysis and model interpretation, ultimately accelerating the machine learning development lifecycle. Automation has emerged as a powerful catalyst in the realm of feature engineering. By automating routine and time-consuming tasks such as data cleaning, feature creation, and selection, data scientists can dedicate more cognitive resources to higher-level problem-solving and model interpretation. This acceleration of the feature engineering process not only improves efficiency but also allows for experimentation with a wider range of feature combinations, ultimately leading to the development of more robust and accurate machine learning models.

CONCLUSION

Feature engineering is the art and science of transforming raw data into meaningful representations that can be effectively utilized by machine learning algorithms. It is a critical step in the data science pipeline that significantly impacts model performance. By carefully selecting, transforming, and creating new features, data scientists can extract valuable insights, improve prediction accuracy, and build robust models. While it requires a combination of domain expertise, statistical knowledge, and computational skills, the rewards of effective feature engineering are substantial, leading to more accurate, interpretable, and reliable models. Feature engineering is the cornerstone of building powerful and effective machine learning models. By transforming raw data into informative features, data scientists unlock the potential of their datasets and drive superior model performance. Data is the lifeblood of the modern world, powering everything from scientific discovery to business operations. Yet, raw data alone is often insufficient for extracting meaningful insights. The quality, relevance, and structure of data are paramount in deriving accurate and actionable knowledge. In today's data-driven landscape, organizations that can effectively harness the power of their data through careful curation and preparation will gain a significant competitive advantage. While it demands a blend of domain expertise, statistical acumen, and computational skills, the rewards are substantial. From enhancing model accuracy and interpretability to mitigating biases, feature engineering is an indispensable component of the data science toolkit. As technology continues to evolve, with advancements in automation and explainability, the future of feature engineering holds immense promise for unlocking even greater insights and driving innovation across industries. Ultimately, the success of a machine learning model hinges on the quality of its features. By investing time and effort into crafting meaningful features, practitioners can significantly increase their chances of building models that deliver real-world impact. By transforming raw data into informative features, we unlock the potential for models to uncover hidden patterns, make accurate predictions, and drive meaningful insights. While the process can be challenging, requiring a blend of domain expertise, statistical knowledge, and computational skills, the rewards are substantial. As the field of machine learning continues to evolve, so too will the techniques and tools for feature engineering. By embracing emerging trends like automation, deep learning, and interpretability, we can unlock even greater potential from our data and create models that deliver exceptional value. Ultimately, the success of any machine learning project hinges on the quality of its features, making feature engineering an indispensable skill for data scientists and analysts alike.

The future of feature engineering promises to be a dynamic landscape, characterized by a deeper integration of human expertise and automation. Data is the lifeblood of modern organizations, serving as the raw material for extracting valuable insights and driving informed decision-making. However, raw data alone is often insufficient. The ability to transform this data into meaningful and actionable information is paramount. This is where the concept of "right data" comes into play. It encompasses not only the collection of relevant data but also its quality, accessibility, and suitability for specific analytical tasks. The journey from raw data to actionable insights requires careful curation, cleaning, and transformation to ensure that the data is fit for purpose. As data volumes and complexity continue to grow, automated feature engineering tools will become increasingly sophisticated, freeing up data scientists to focus on higher-level tasks. However, raw data is often unstructured, noisy, and incomplete, limiting its potential value. To unlock the true power of data, it must be transformed into a format that can be consumed and analyzed by machines. This process, known as data preparation, involves a series of steps that clean, structure, and enrich data, ultimately creating high-quality datasets ready for analysis and modeling. Simultaneously, there will be a growing emphasis on interpretability and explainability, necessitating the development of techniques that shed light on the inner workings of complex models. Moreover, domain-specific feature engineering will gain prominence as industries recognize the value of tailoring features to their unique challenges and opportunities.

## CHAPTER THIRTEEN

REFERENCES

[1] M. Anderson, D. Antenucci, V. Bittorf, M. Burgess, M. J. Cafarella, A. Kumar, F. Niu, Y. Park, C. Ré, and C. Zhang, "Brainwash: A Data System for Feature Engineering.," in Proc. CIDR 2013, 2013.

[2] P. Domingos, "A few useful things to know about machine learning," Commun. ACM, vol. 55, no. 10, pp. 78–87, 2012.

[3] Isabell Guyon and André Elisseeff, 2006. "An Introduction to Feature Extraction," in Guyon, Isabelle, Steve Gunn, Masoud Nikravesh, and Lofti A. Zadeh, eds. Feature Extraction: Foundations and Applications, pp. 1-25. Springer Berlin Heidelberg, 2006.

[4] J. Cheng and M. S. Bernstein, "Flock: Hybrid Crowd-Machine Learning Classifiers," 2015, pp. 600–611.

[5] P. Domingos, "A few useful things to know about machine learning," Commun. ACM, vol. 55, no. 10, pp. 78–87, 2012.

[6] https://en.wikipedia.org/wiki/feature-engineering.

[7] What is the intuitive explanation of feature engineering in ML?-Quora, www.quora.com. Retrieved, 2015-11-11.

[8] S. Bird, E. Klein, and E. Loper, Natural Language Processing with Python. O'Reilly Media, Inc., 2009.

[9] H. Raghavan, O. Madani, and R. Jones, "InterActive Feature Selection," in Proc. IJCAI 2005, 2005, vol. 5

[10] J. Cheng and M. S. Bernstein, "Flock: Hybrid Crowd-Machine Learning Classifiers," 2015, pp. 600–611

[11] F. Heimerl, C. Jochim, S. Koch, and T. Ertl, "FeatureForge: A Novel Tool for Visually Supported Feature Engineering and Corpus

Revision," in Proceedings of COLING 2012: Posters, Mumbai, India, 2012, pp. 461–470.

[12] Scott Sam, Matwin Stan, Feature Engineering for Text Classification, Proceedings of ICML-99, 16th International Conference on Machine Learning,1999

[13] Gabor Berand, Richard Farkas, SZTERGAK: Feature Engineering for Keyphrase Extraction, Proceedings of the 5th International Workshop

on Semantic Evaluation, p. 186-189, July 15-16, 2010, Los Angeles, California.

[14] Cramer, S., Kampouridis, M., Freitas, A.A., Feature Engineering for Improving Financial Derivatives-based Rainfall Prediction, IEEE World Congress on Computational Intelligence, Vancouver, Canada (2016).

[15] F. Adafre and M. de Rijke. 2005. Feature engineering and post-processing for temporal expression recognition using conditional random fields. In Proceedings of the ACL Workshop on Feature Engineering for Machine Learning in Natural Language Processing.

[16] Jeyanthi Narasimhan, Lawrence Holder, Feature Engineering for Supervised Link Prediction on Dynamic Social Networks, School of Electrical Engineering and Computer Science, Washington State University, Pullman, WA 99164-2752, USA, 7 Oct. 2014.

[17] Kalyan Veeramachaneni , Una-May O'Reilly , Colin Taylor Towards Feature Engineering at Scale for data from Massive open Online Courses, arXiv:1407.5238v1 [cs.CY] 20 Jul 2014.

[18] Christopher Re, Amir Abbas Sadhgein, Zifei Shan, Jaeho Shin, Feiran Wang, Sen Wu, Ce Zhang, Feature Engineering for knowledge Base construction(KBC), Copyright 2014 IEEE. International Journal of Innovations in Engineering and Technology (IJIET) http://dx.doi.org/10.21172/ijiet.82.024 Volume 8 Issue 2 April 2017 179 ISSN: 2319 - 1058

[19] Dai, H.J., Touray, M., Jonnagaddala, J., Syed-Abdul, S.: Feature engineering for recognizing adverse drug reactions from

Twitter posts Information 7(2), 27 (2016).

[20] Bahnsen A. C., et al. (2016). Feature engineering strategies for credit card fraud detection. Expert Systems with Applications, Vol. 51, pp. 134-142.

[21] Wang Christopher Alex, Feature Factory: A Collaborative, Crowd-Sourced Machine learning System, Massachusetts Institute of Technology

## CHAPTER FOURTEEN

ABOUT AUTHORS

1. Dr. N. Krishnaraj is Working as Associate Professor in Networking and Communications Department in SRM Institute of Science and Technology.
2. Dr. M. Sivakumar is Working as Assistant Professor in Networking and Communications Department in SRM Institute of Science and Technology
3. Dr. M. Maranco is Working as Assistant Professor in Networking and Communications Department in SRM Institute of Science and Technology
4. Dr. P. Savaridaasan is Working as Assistant Professor in Networking and Communications Department in SRM Institute of Science and Technology

www.ingramcontent.com/pod-product-compliance
Lightning Source LLC
Chambersburg PA
CBHW040818120726
48005CB00012B/1455